AN INTRODUCTION TO CHURCH COMMUNICATION

Text copyright © 1994 Richard Thomas

The author asserts the moral right
to be identified as the author of this work

Published by
Lynx Communications
Sandy Lane West, Oxford, England
ISBN 0 7459 2886 2
Albatross Books Pty Ltd
PO Box 320, Sutherland, NSW 2232, Australia
ISBN 0 7324 0834 2

First edition 1994

All rights reserved

A catalogue record for this book is available
from the British Library

Printed and bound in Malta by Interprint Ltd.

AN INTRODUCTION TO CHURCH COMMUNICATION

Richard Thomas

LYNX

CONTENTS

FOREWORD		**7**
INTRODUCTION		**8**

SECTION ONE – A COMMUNICATIONS PLAN

1	GETTING PERMISSION	14
2	CONSTRUCTING A COMMUNICATIONS PLAN	18
3	COLLECTING THE DATA	24
4	DEFINING YOUR COMMUNICATION AIMS	27
5	PEOPLE, TIME AND MONEY	31
6	IDENTIFYING THOSE YOU WANT TO REACH	37
7	WHAT RESPONSE DO YOU WANT?	40
8	MEASURING THE RESULTS	43
9	CHOOSING THE MEDIA	47
10	DEFINING THE MESSAGE	51
11	EXECUTING THE PLAN	56
12	MEASURING THE RESULTS	61

SECTION TWO – MEDIA OPTIONS

13	THE MEDIA AT YOUR DISPOSAL	68
14	GAINING ACCESS TO THE PRINTED AND BROADCAST MEDIA	71

15	TELEVISION AS A MEDIUM	78
16	RADIO AS A MEDIUM	84
17	NEWSPAPERS AS A MEDIUM	89
18	DEALING WITH BAD NEWS	95
19	POSTERS AND LEAFLETS	99
20	THE CHURCH MAGAZINE	102
21	ADVERTISING	111
22	FREEPOST, RESPONSE MECHANISMS AND DIRECT MAIL	116
23	DISPLAYS, EXHIBITIONS, NOTICE-BOARDS	120
24	COORDINATING YOUR MEDIA CHOICES	123

SECTION THREE – COMMUNICATION THEORY

25	UNDERSTANDING COMMUNICATION SYSTEMS	130
26	COMMUNICATION BETWEEN SYSTEMS	137
27	WORKING WITH TEAMS	143
28	IMAGE AND MYTH	148
29	TAIL PIECE	152

FOREWORD

Communication is vital for all churches. First, we have good news to share. Too often, what we say comes across as stale news or bad news or as so little newsworthy that it fails to communicate at all.

Secondly, the churches are now news in a way that they have not been for some time. But so often they are depicted in a bad light. The Church of England, in particular, is depicted as being on the skids.

In order to communicate the gospel and in order to present the church in a better light, we need all the wisdom and skills we can find. Richard Thomas has these. For five years he has been Communications Officer of the Diocese of Oxford and has performed this task in a highly professional way. He sees communication as belonging to the church as a whole and affecting every aspect of our life.

I warmly commend *An Introduction to Church Communication* as a clear, authoritative and challenging read for all those concerned that the Christian church should communicate its message more effectively and convincingly.

Richard Harries, Bishop of Oxford

INTRODUCTION

The aim of this book is to help you learn the practice of Christian communication. Maybe your church has put you in charge of 'the publicity'; maybe you're a church leader wanting to improve your church's communication; perhaps you're a student preparing for ministry; or maybe you're just interested in the subject. Whatever your reason, you'll find that a clearer understanding of church communication will help both mission and pastoral care. If you follow carefully the process set out in this book, you will find that it takes you through the stages of planning so that you end up with a carefully designed communication plan that you can execute with confidence.

THE STARTING POINT

God wasn't born in a stable in Bethlehem merely to convey information. Our message is not about God: God himself is the message. As John says: 'That which was from the beginning, which we have heard, which we have seen with our eyes, which we have looked at and our hands have touched—this we proclaim concerning the Word of life.' Jesus didn't simply convey a message. He transmits life itself, and everyone he touches is transformed, changed, made more fully alive. His stories acted, and still act today, like yeast in a dough. They work in us, expanding our vision, shattering our illusions and bringing us to life.

Our communication does not begin with a decision by a committee or a church council to activate a particular message. Our communication begins with the activity of the Holy Spirit driving us forward, 'into all truth', as John puts it. The initiative is God's. As the proverb says: 'Many are the plans in a man's heart, but it is the Lord's purpose that prevails.'

That's what makes Christian communication unique. We begin with neither a product, nor with a message—we begin with the God who is alive and present in his people, and who longs to bring others into a living relationship with himself. Or rather, God begins with us!

But the mystery goes deeper still. Secular communication may be neutral, a bridge across which we transmit messages, information and requests. More often it is a biased vehicle, colouring its messages with a political or commercial purpose. It can even be hostile, conveying hidden messages, manipulating by technique or psychological persuasion. But our model is that of the cross. For us, communication which alienates, or manipulates by hidden persuasion, is contrary to the gospel. Ours is the God who emptied himself, taking the form of a servant in order to bring others into a relationship with himself. The willingness to put yourself at risk, to be open to rejection and misunderstanding, because you are yourself part of the message, is something that few secular communicators will understand. You can present the gospel by living it and by doing your best to communicate it, but there will still be times when the message is not only rejected, but deliberately misunderstood. Jesus was the greatest communicator who ever lived, and look what they did to him.

But if you want to say something as intimate and as all-consuming as 'I love you', you can hardly avoid being personally involved. The analogy of the lover is important. Its not just what you say, and what you do, that conveys the message. There are times when silence is important. Sometimes the agony of deciding not to phone, or when to keep quiet, is what builds the relationship. Jesus knew this, and often warned his disciples about it. 'Go. And tell no-one', he said to the blind man he had just healed. 'Don't cast your pearls before swine.' And when asked why he spoke in the riddle of parables, he answered with yet another riddle: 'So that they may hear, and hear, but not understand.' Those who know the theology of the remnant in Isaiah will immediately recognize the meaning. But for the rest of us, well, it can sometimes seem almost perverse. Here is someone with a tremendous message, yet he speaks in riddles, and is almost determined not to make it clear. And then we go and spend time and money hurling pearls at swine, and feeling guilty because we feel ever so slightly embarrassed.

The mystery, the 'hidden-ness' of the gospel, is as important to the Christian communicator as 'spreading the word'. The wise communicator knows by instinct, or possibly through the Holy Spirit, when to speak out and when to keep quiet. Sometimes this is the most difficult choice of all; not defining the communication aim, but simply deciding that, this time, the best communication is silence: creating the space in which the Holy Spirit can work best. This is not a skill that can be taught, or a trick of professional judgment: it is only something that comes as we walk closely with God. It comes through prayer. And its expression is often part of the cost of discipleship.

THE DISCIPLINES

It would be wrong to think that we have nothing to learn from secular communication practices, however. There are certain disciplines which are common to us all simply because they reflect the way God made us. If we ignore them, then we simply waste time, money and energy. In fact, the first law of Christian communication might be stated:

Good communication costs time, money and energy.

Bad communication wastes time, money and energy.

And, you might add: 'Usually other people's!' I was once asked to review 'the publicity' of a large church mission. I was shown leaflet after leaflet on just about every aspect of the mission you could imagine. The church members would (if they had time to read it all) be very informed about everything from car parking to counselling. But there was nothing at all for those who were not members of the church! When I asked them who they planned to invite to the mission, they were rather taken aback. The very first principle of communication—'who do you want to reach?'—had not been addressed, and they had spent hundreds of pounds, hours of work and masses of energy entirely on internal communication—literally preaching to the converted!

The second law of Christian communication might be stated like this:

> **Good communication gets things done—it improves morale, and assists church growth.**

> **Bad communication stops things being done—it lowers morale, and empties churches.**

If you think this is overstating the case, here's an example of what can happen when the most simple internal communication goes wrong.

The church youth group decide to hold an 'outreach disco'. They decide that Thursday evening is the best evening to get their friends along, but in the heat of planning they forget to check on the availability of the Church Hall. When the Women's Circle begin to arrive for their regular Thursday evening meeting, they find laser lights and music loud enough to mask the sound of a Jumbo Jet on full thrust. In a spirit of Christian love, they agree to hold their meeting at Mrs Jones' house.

The disco is a roaring success. But when, the following Thursday, the Women's Circle turn up for their meeting to find an 'outreach rock concert' in full swing, the spirit of Christian love fails, Mrs Jones says she will leave the church, and Mrs Smith, determined to 'have it out' with the young people, disrupts the outreach rather badly.

Communication and administration are very closely related. That's not surprising when you recognize the close relationship between communion and ministry. Where the internal communication of a church, or a church group, is good, then everyone feels that they belong, that they have a place and a task, and that things are really going well.

It's not only the external communication of mission that motivates us to improve our communication: improving our internal communication will help our churches to grow, and can be a powerful factor in good discipleship.

It doesn't matter whether the task is to improve the communications within a church, a diocese, a house group, a deacons' meeting or the youth fellowship: the starting point is always the same. It's the desire to bring people into relationship. Not just any old relationship, but one that is warm, affirming, healing and free from manipulation. The sort of relationship that Jesus had with his disciples, and one that the Holy Spirit forms in us today.

It's a point that's easy to forget, as we busy ourselves with the techniques of media management, with communication strategies, with publicity for this or that. The test that can be applied to any aspect of Christian communication is whether or not it is bringing people into a warmer, deeper, richer relationship with the God who loves them and with the people he has redeemed; whether it is furthering 'Shalom', the well-being of God's love. Throughout this book we'll be stressing the need to measure, to test and to reflect on data we have gathered either formally or informally. But as we start the process of learning how to communicate effectively, it's worth stressing the most important test of all: is what we're doing helping or hindering the formation of deep, Spirit-filled relationships?

If we can apply that test to ourselves and our work, and be at peace with the answer, then no matter how hard the task, how difficult the job or how long the journey, we will not have strayed too far from the track. And if, as must happen from time to time, especially in the stressful environment of dealing with the press, running a publicity campaign or making important changes, we get it wrong, upset someone, or behave in a way that does not glorify our Father, there is always the opportunity to forgive and to be forgiven.

So let's make a start. This book is set out in a carefully designed way to take you through the steps needed to get your communications right, so it's important that you understand its shape. The first section deals with the basic design of a communications plan. It includes both external communication (with those who are not church members) and internal communications (with those who are members). Chapter 1 deals with getting permission and ownership, and Chapter 2 outlines the steps needed. Chapters 3–12 look at those steps in detail. Simply following those steps will produce a communications plan that will produce results.

The second section (Chapters 13–24) deals with the various media options you might choose to include in your plan, how they work, and how to use them effectively. These include: newspapers, radio, TV, posters, leaflets, etc.; what they can and can't do; creating your own media, working with journalists; running a press conference and writing press releases; the cost-effective use of advertising (independent radio, newspaper, television, trade and local publications); using freepost and business reply; direct mail; notice boards and sign posting; the church magazine and its production, distribution, and funding, and of course, the individual himself or herself. Finally, Chapter 24 shows how to put these various choices together into a comprehensive media selection.

The third section deals exclusively with the theory behind the practice. This includes: the system and how it works; communication between and within systems; why systems break down and what the symptoms are when a system is not functioning properly. The book concludes with a chapter on image, and the importance of being able to communicate with those whose image of the church is less than accurate.

TAIL-PIECE

I said earlier that Jesus didn't come just to convey information. He comes to bring life itself. And he comes through the life of the Spirit, 'the go-between God' (to use Bishop John Taylor's phrase) whose task it is to bring us into all truth. It's easy when learning any discipline to fear that you are substituting the deadness of human laws for the Spirit's vitality. But 'discipline' is all about becoming a disciple. If you want to play the violin so that the most inspired music can flow effortlessly from your heart, there are rules to be learned and scales to be practised. And if you want to communicate that vitality which is at the heart of God himself, then it can help to learn the disciplines of good communication. It will cost you time, energy and money. But remember the alternative!

SECTION ONE

A COMMUNICATIONS PLAN

1 GETTING PERMISSION

By whose authority do you do these things?

In the days of the great sailing ships, cannons were held in place by ropes. The ropes were there to keep the cannons pointing in the right direction so that the shot hit the target, and also to prevent injury to the sailors who manned them. Above all, the ropes were there to absorb the stresses and strains of recoil. But occasionally a rope would break and the cannon would get 'loose'. It could then leap backwards, swing round in the gun-deck, and fire into the ship itself, almost always causing injury.

There is no room for a 'loose cannon' in the work of the church. The person who takes it upon himself or herself to 'improve' communications without getting the necessary agreement is in danger of causing more harm than good. It certainly won't help if you start moving people's notices around the notice-board because you believe it needs 'tidying'. Nor will it help much if you take it upon yourself to send a press release to the local paper without the agreement of the event organizer. Having been the victim of this kind of 'help', I can say with good authority that it causes extra work, confusion and bad feeling. Not only that, but if you act from division, you will communicate division. Not the best message for the church to give to the world.

It may be that things are desperately in need of improvement. It may be that you not only know what needs doing, but have the professional skill to improve things. But you still need to resist the temptation to act on your own.

The place to start is by making a proposal to the leadership of your church. You might raise the issue at a church meeting, or write a paper for the elders. You could even ask a few church members whether they would agree to support your suggestions. But you will need to get approval.

This isn't just a matter of church discipline, but of good communication practice. The church is a community called into being by God. Each member is important, and is as likely to reflect God's will for his church as the next. St Benedict, who founded the monastic movement that was to keep Christianity alive through the Dark Ages, and which was to evangelize much of Western Europe, knew this well. He wrote in his *Rule* which governed the monastic communities:

When anything important has to be done in the monastery the Abbot must assemble the whole community and explain what is under consideration. When he has heard the counsel of the brethren, he should give it consideration and then take what seems to him the best course. The reason why we say that all should be called to council is this: It is often to a younger brother that the Lord reveals the best course. But the brethren must give their counsel submissively and humbly and not presume stubbornly to defend their opinions.

Rule of St Benedict, chapter 3

The mission and ministry of the community depended on having a common mind: often that mind had to be expressed by the leadership, but only after prayerful consideration of even the most junior members. St Benedict continues:

No one in the monastery is to follow the prompting of his own heart; no one is to presume to argue rudely with the Abbot, or to argue at all outside the monastery.

There was room for individuals to express concerns, to challenge the direction of the community, or to put issues on the agenda for the community. What was not allowed was anyone going off and doing 'their own thing'. Loose cannons were not welcome!

HOW TO GET AGREEMENT TO DEVELOP A COMMUNICATIONS PLAN

It is important to get agreement from the church to address a problem of communication. It can be a daunting task. But if you follow a step-by-step plan such as the one outlined in Chapter 2, it should not be too difficult. Remember, things take time. In the New Testament there are two words for time: *chronos*, which means the simple minute-by-minute progression of time, and *kairos*, which means the right time, the appropriate moment. You will need both. Remember the first rule: good communication costs time, money and energy. So here's one way that you might approach the problem:

◆ set out the problem or difficulty as you see it

◆ suggest a process to address those problems or difficulties

◆ agree a time-scale

◆ identify the human and financial resources you will need

◆ get support from the people who give informal approval

◆ get formal approval from the appropriate group.

Notice that nothing is said about solutions—yet. One of the quickest ways of getting stuck or setting off down the wrong road is to start off by suggesting solutions before the problem has been properly identified and analysed. There will be data to collect, reflections to be made and, possibly, model solutions to be piloted, before anyone can be sure that the solution they are proposing even begins to meet the problem.

SET OUT THE PROBLEM AS YOU SEE IT

This need not necessarily take long, but it does need to be done. And it needs to be done in a way that doesn't place blame on individuals or their work, or seek to denigrate other members of the community. It helps to start off with the good things, with encouragement. For example, the beginning of a proposal to improve communication with young people could start like this:

The youth fellowship is making no attempt to communicate with young people who don't come to church, and consequently it is stagnating...

But it would be much better if it started like this:

The church has done a great deal recently to improve its work with young people, and many of our existing youth fellowship have said how much the club nights have improved...

Having set the context, you then need to explain the problem as you see it:

However, we are still failing to attract new members from beyond the families of those who already come to church. With such committed leadership, it is a pity that our communication with young people outside the church is not better...

Having stated the problem, you now need to suggest a way to deal with it. Remember, it's no good at this stage suggesting a solution. There's a lot of work to be done yet:

It would be unfair to ask the youth leaders to take on any more work. I therefore propose that we set up a small working group to look at ways of improving our communication with young people who don't come to church. I am willing to lead such a group, and would suggest that it comes back with suggestions in about eight weeks' time.

It helps if the proposal can also say who might take part, and whether the group will need any money. For example:

I would like to invite two young people from the youth fellowship to work with me, and I would like approval to spend up to ...... on research. The group will work closely with the leaders of the youth fellowship.

GET SUPPORT FROM THE PEOPLE WHO GIVE INFORMAL APPROVAL

In every community there will be people who, because of the role they take or the position they hold, will have a powerful influence on the outcome of any discussion. Their support for your proposal may not be conclusive, but it will help a great deal. Without their support, it will be much harder to gain formal approval. With their support, formal approval might be made a great deal easier, and they might be able to offer suggestions that will improve your proposal considerably. Besides, no one likes management by surprise.

GET FORMAL APPROVAL FROM THE APPROPRIATE GROUP

Having gained the informal support of the minister, elder or deacon, there will need to be formal approval for the work you intend to do. In most cases it's easy to discover which body needs to give approval, and if it's unclear, then the minister or elder will be able to guide you. But it's essential that before any major work is done, the church has given formal approval.

It can also be done the other way round. The church might be holding a mission, or some other fairly major event, and might have approached you to 'do the publicity'. The approval process applies just as much to work which the church itself wants to initiate. Unless you get them to agree the terms of the job, both you and the church committee could end up with a nasty surprise. At best, you will be unsure of your boundaries, and the job will take longer. And quite often, the discussion about precisely what is required throws up all sorts of issues and limitations that the enthusiasm of the moment had overlooked. One church I knew asked for help with its publicity for a fairly major event, but when we asked what budget was available for printing and advertising, we were told rather sheepishly that there was nothing set aside for this aspect of the work! It pays to check.

GETTING A TEAM TOGETHER

As with most things, working as part of a team is infinitely preferable to going it alone. There may be a group of two or three people who have the energy to work with you for a defined period of time, or you may need to recruit. We go into detail about team selection and building in Section 3 of the book, but for now, I will assume that your team is in place, your proposal has been agreed and authorized, and you are ready to start.

2 CONSTRUCTING A COMMUNICATIONS PLAN

The first step in any professional communication is to design a communications plan that will translate a clearly defined communication aim into a practical set of actions that can be measured and that will get the desired results. Sadly, in many churches the plan is defined, if it is defined at all, something like this:

Step 1 I have something to say.

Step 2 I say it.

Step 3 Why haven't you responded?

We are rightly keen to get the message across. After all, that's what Christian communication is all about. We have a tremendous message, and we're going to get it across! Most of us think that because we learned to talk almost before we learned to walk, we can communicate. But sadly, that's not always true.

The message we're trying to communicate could be completely inappropriate for the people we are trying to reach. It could be couched in a language they can't understand. It might assume knowledge that is not there.

This morning I want to expound to you the propitiatory or expiatory atonement for the state of man's carnal separation...!

Equally, the medium might be inappropriate either for the message or for the people we are trying to reach. You wouldn't try to reach children by writing a letter to the quality newspapers. And it is not helpful preaching a sermon about poor church attendance to those few people who have taken the trouble to turn up!

Communication needs to be planned in much the same way that any other aspect of the life of the church needs to be planned.

We recently took the decision to build a new church. It was to be on a newly established housing estate, and had to serve a Christian fellowship that had outgrown the small room which had served as the base for a church-plant a few years earlier. But it wasn't just for the Christian fellowship: it also had to serve the community in which it was set. The first thing the architect did after his appointment was to sit down with a group of us and let us talk about the type of building we thought we needed. We described all the ideas we had, the vision for outreach and pastoral care. We told him how we worshipped, how we worked with our children. We explained how the building would need to be used during the week, but how we needed somewhere for daily prayer. We drew sketches and dreamed dreams.

The next thing the architect did was to look at the site for the new building. He took photographs. He talked to people who lived nearby. He got the 'feel' of the area. He talked informally to the planning authority.

And only after he had done all this could he start drawing. We continued to meet with him, discussing his ideas, rejecting some, welcoming others. And slowly the plan for the new church took shape. When he thought it was about right, he made a model out of card and showed it to the fellowship, explaining what each room was for and how it might be used. We loved his ideas, but more than that, we began to feel that this was 'our' new church. It already felt as though we had started to occupy it. And when the small matter of the cost of the new church was raised, it was almost a foregone conclusion that the money would be there.

Before any foundation was dug, or any brick laid, hours of work had been done on designing the plans. That was the important stage. The building was merely a matter of interpreting the drawing, turning them into walls, doors and windows. There was no way we could have gone straight to the building stage without this careful preparation, without a plan to follow, and the strength of the Christian fellowship behind us.

If we take that much care over the plans to build a building, how much more care should we put into building the structures of the living church? Yet so often we go straight to the implementation of a hastily thought-out plan, without discussing it with the leadership, without sharing our vision with the Christian fellowship, or trying to ensure that our aims meet the needs of the people we are serving.

If the communication structures of our church, our fellowship, our college or the mission we are running are not carefully thought out, planned, discussed and agreed, its unlikely that they will work properly. Money will be spent badly, and time will be wasted.

Good communication costs time, money and energy.

Bad communication wastes time, money and energy.

STEPS IN DESIGNING A COMMUNICATIONS PLAN.

Step 1 Collect the information you need.

Step 2 Define your communication aims.

Step 3 Agree the budget, resources and time-scale.

Step 4 Decide who you want to communicate with.

Step 5 Agree the response you want.

Step 6 Decide what the success factors will be.

Step 7 Decide who the messages should come from.

Step 8 Choose the appropriate media.

Step 9 Define the messages.

Step 10 Execute the plan.

Step 11 Measure the results.

Step 1 Collect the information you need

You're going to need information about what is happening now, where the organization is at the moment, what its hopes and aspirations are for its communications, and what level of resources and activity it is used to providing. Most important, you will need information about the vision of the community or organization.

Collecting this information, or data, can be done informally by chatting to people, looking around, holding a briefing meeting, or using a more formal questionnaire approach. But it is an essential first step. We cover the various data-collection methods in Chapter 3.

Step 2 Define your communication aims

This should be a clear statement of the overall task, and it can usually be written down in one or two sentences. One way of getting used to writing a clear communication aim is to say: 'We want to do this so that that will happen.' Communication aims are covered in detail in Chapter 4.

Step 3 Agree the budget, resources and time-scale

Good communication costs time, money and energy. You will need to know how much of each you have to work with. For example, what skills are you likely to need and can you find people with those skills? What is a reasonable length of time to achieve the task without losing people's enthusiasm? How much money is available to do the job? We look at resources in Chapter 5.

Step 4 Decide who you want to communicate with

Your aim may be broad, but you need to be very specific in listing all the groups of people who need to respond. In fact, you're likely to need two lists: one for the various groups of people who belong to your organization (the internal communication list), and one for the various groups of people who do not belong (the external communication list). We look at targeted communication in Chapter 6.

Step 5 Agree the response you want

There is almost always a response required from any communication exercise. That's why the money is being spent and why the time is being given. And if you are not clear what that response should be, how can you define a plan which will achieve it, or even communicate it clearly? Again, it helps to write it down. We look at response definitions in Chapter 7.

Step 6 Decide what the success factors will be

We will look in depth at the question 'Why bother to measure?' in Chapter 8. But if you're going to have any real measure of how effective your use of time and money has been, now is the time to decide what constitutes success. For example, if you want to promote your church's work with mothers and toddlers, you might suggest that if 50 per cent of the mums in your area know of the work, you will have succeeded. It is a good discipline to account for the time and money you spend, particularly as it's not your own!

Step 7 Decide who the messages should come from

The originator of the message is a vital element in getting the message valued or even received. You might value the views of your taxi driver on the state of the health service, but you might be a little more reluctant to take his advice about your health! The credibility and appropriateness of the originator is essential to the value of the message.

Step 8 Choose the appropriate media

Here's a new proverb: The man who tries to communicate with teenagers by writing an article in the parish magazine may have a long wait! True, communicating with some groups is more difficult than with others, but it helps to choose an appropriate medium. It's very probable that you will need more than one, and that you will have to make some choices about which should take priority. We look at how to choose the right media in Chapter 9.

Step 9 Define the messages

Only now are you ready to decide on the precise messages you will send. They will come from an originator you have carefully chosen, they will be transmitted by media that is appropriate to the target group, and they will be designed to get the required response. Chapter 10 deals with defining your message.

Step 10 Execute the plan

By now, the communication plan should be so well structured that, like a train running down a railway track, it just keeps going until it gets to where it wants to be. If only life were like that. In practice, there will always be unforeseen problems, and the pressure to make last-minute changes. Knowing when to keep your nerve and when to accept the need for change is a fine art. We look at some of the issues in Chapter 11.

Step 11 Measure the results

This is where your success factors come into play. You may choose to measure in steps along the way, or simply to measure the end result of your work. But if you forget to do this, you will never be able to answer the question: 'Well, how did it all go?' And those who complain that too much money was spent, or even that not enough was spent, will be able to have an objective measure to test your answer against. You, of course, will be able to step back from criticism and self-doubt by the simple process of pointing to the results. If they are good, then no explanation is needed. If they are not, then the measurements can be used to examine what went wrong. Either way, you are in a better position. Measurement is covered in Chapter 12.

INTERNAL AND EXTERNAL COMMUNICATION

A good sailor keeps an eye on two things: the compass and the barometer. The compass tells him what is happening to the conditions he can control. He can make changes to his course, instruct his crew or change his sails to get the best course and speed. The barometer tells him what is happening outside his boat and outside his control, what weather to be expected, and what effect it might have on the course he wants to steer.

So too a good communicator keeps his or her eye on both internal and external communications. Internal communication is that communication that takes place with those who belong to the organization, church or group. It is 'internal' to the system (see Section 3 of the book for an explanation of systems and how they work).

External communication is that which takes place with those who do not belong to the organization, church or group. It takes place across the boundaries of the system, and often has to penetrate into different cultures and assumptions.

> **Internal communication takes place with the members of the organization.**

> **External communication takes place with those who are not members of the organization.**

It is easy to neglect either of these by concentrating too hard on the other. But in most communications plans, both internal and external communication have to be built into the structure.

CLARIFYING THE BOUNDARIES

If we're going to be clear about the design of the communications plan, it helps to be clear about whose plan it is. On whose behalf are you doing this work? Is it being done because you think it needs doing, or because someone has asked you? Does the person who suggested the work belong to the organization, or are they suggesting from the 'outside'? In short, what is your place in the system?

At first, this might seem to be splitting hairs. But consider the following story:

Susan was a member of a fellowship in her village. She also worked for a marketing company which sent her on a course to improve her communication skills. Her boss, who lived in the same village but who was not a member of her fellowship, said to her at the end of the course: 'Now you'll be able to do something about those awful newsletters that your church keeps putting through our letterboxes.' The remark hurt, because Susan helped every three months to put the outreach newsletter together. The fellowship had been quite proud of the result, but after going on the course, she began to see all sorts of things that could be 'improved'.

The next meeting of the outreach group went badly. Susan kept making suggestions to 'improve' things, and the others kept turning down her ideas. At home after the meeting, Susan decided to try once again. She put together a mock-up of a different, 'improved' newsletter and sent it to the leader of the outreach group. He came to see her, and explained that, glad as they were for her suggestions, the group was very happy with the original version. Susan was a member of the fellowship. But she got so cross about their refusal to do things 'professionally' that she left.

For further information on boundaries, what they are and how to set them and keep them intact, see Chapter 25.

3 COLLECTING THE DATA

The first thing anyone is going to need in order to begin to plan a communications strategy is information. They're going to need information about what is needed, where the organization is at the moment, what its hopes and aspirations are for its communication, and what level of resource and activity it is used to providing. They're going to need to know which groups of people are opposed to change, and where they might get support for change. Above all, they're going to need to know what vision the church or organization has for the future.

TAKE A LOOK AROUND

There's two ways to collect information, or data. The first is by some formal process such as a focus group (qualitative research) which searches out issues and attitudes, or a survey (quantitative research) which measures percentages and numbers. Often, a number of focus groups are set up to discover attitudes and issues, and then these are used as a basis for testing a representative sample to find out how many people hold those attitudes or are concerned about those issues. The other is by a more informal, subjective process. Even if it's intended to set up formal qualitative research as a basis for a quantitative survey, it's a good idea to get some general impression about the organization concerned. So let's make a start.

Take a general look around. Even if you are tackling only a small part of your church's communications, it will help to set it in context. You could do this on your own, or it could be the first task of a newly created communication team. It can be done with pencil, paper and clipboard, but it's probably best done informally, with an awareness of the messages you are getting about how people are feeling. Later on, we'll look at formal data collection, communication surveys and planning. But first impressions, especially when they come fresh, can be very important and I usually try to absorb as many clues as possible from a first, informal visit.

Unless the task is a really small one, you will need to start with the building. Look at its setting. What are the buildings like surrounding it? What messages come from the context in which its placed? Is it in a new housing estate, or set in a picturesque rural village? Listen to your feelings. What do they tell you? Is the building in good repair? Does it look well cared-for? What does the state of the grass or the fence tell you? Is

COLLECTING THE DATA

there a notice-board or a sign which says what the building is and what happens inside it? Is the paint peeling?

Go into the building and take a look around. What messages did you get from your eyes, ears and feelings when you walked through the door? Could you go in at all, or was the door locked? What information is available for the visitor? Would they be able to find help easily?

Join God's people for worship. Again, use your eyes, your ears and your feelings to monitor the messages you receive. How do you feel when you first walk in? What books or leaflets are you given? How do you know where to sit? What was your impression of the worship? Could you hear properly? Was it clear what you were expected to do? If you're the minister it might help to ask someone else to do this exercise for you, but let them tell you honestly what they found.

The next step is to meet the people themselves. Of course, if you're one of them and you worship there regularly, you'll know them already. But this time as you chat with them, listen carefully not only to what they're saying, but what other messages they give underneath the words. What was the conversation about? How did you feel?

You will have picked up broad hints, clues about information that was missing, and about expectations that were not fully explained. There will be some things that will strike you as being particularly good, or affirming, or helpful. Remember those things, because later on you'll probably need to do some affirming yourself.

If this preliminary look at the context of the church and its ministry is taken seriously, sufficient clues will have been picked up for the communicator to begin to form an idea about not only the things that might need doing, but also about ways of tackling the issues.

FORMAL DATA COLLECTION, SURVEYS AND PLANNING

There are two main forms of data collection: qualitative, which is concerned with identifying common concerns, issues, thoughts or feelings; and quantitative, which measures the number of people who subscribe to these concerns, issues, thoughts or feelings. Qualitative research identifies areas of common concern, whilst quantitative research, like an opinion poll, measures numbers.

Qualitative research is usually done by getting together at least six 'focus' groups carefully chosen to represent a cross-section of the people to be surveyed. The enabler guides a conversation aimed at getting the groups' views about the subjects to be researched. Considerable skill is needed to guide the conversations, which are usually taped, and to interpret the answers. Qualitative research of strangers is not something that should be attempted by amateurs, but there is no reason why the communicator should not get together an informal group of people to discuss the priorities or communication needs of a church or group, and this can be a good starting point.

A quantitative survey often bases its questions on the results of qualitative research. Carefully phrased 'closed' questions are asked, and 'yes' or 'no' answers recorded, or a respondent's position in a range of options is noted. With careful thought, quantitative surveys can provide a church with a great deal of information. The next step is getting a proposal together, and getting it approved by the church.

Stephen wanted to know what the local community knew about his church. He'd offered to do some work on improving the church's communication, so he drew up a simple questionnaire designed to find out what people living in the area knew about the church and what it offered. He found that few people knew about the work it was doing with young children, and many people, when asked about what they wanted the church to provide, said that they wanted more provision for children!

There was clearly a communication gap between what the church was already providing in its work with young children, and what the community knew about that work. So he set out a communications plan aimed at informing the local community about his church's work with young people.

DEFINING YOUR COMMUNICATION AIMS

WHAT IS A COMMUNICATION AIM?

A communication aim is a statement about what is to be achieved with a particular programme or communication project, and it is used as to measure the success or failure of the communication programme. A good communication aim is usually short, sharp and specific. It says what is to be done, why it's to be done, and for how long. It should be agreed by the church, or group, on whose behalf the work is being done, and it should be realistic and achievable within the resources of time and money available.

A statement of the communication aim can take some time and discussion before it is complete.

The minister in charge of St James's Church sat down with his communications director to discuss plans for publicity for the forthcoming mission. Their first attempt at a communication aim was this:

We aim to communicate with people about the mission.

It certainly says what is to be done, but in a very broad way. There is nothing about why it's being done, nor about the time-scale within which it's to be done. It isn't specific enough, either. 'We' is far too undefined, as is 'people'. They tried again.

During the six months leading up to the mission, we aim to communicate with everyone living in the parish so that they know about the mission.

That's certainly better. It contains a statement about time-scale, it defines the target group by geographical area, and defines the required result. But there are still several areas of weakness. The first concerns the definition of the target group. Are they sure that they only want to communicate with those who live in the parish, or are there others who might be interested? Ideas for the mission include a business lunch, so what about those who come in every day to work there?

The second, and more serious fault, is in the statement about the desired result. Are they really going to spend six months and a lot of money so that people will merely 'know' about the mission? Or do they really want people to come along, take part, get involved?

Failing to define the desired result is, in my experience, one of the most common communication faults in any church. The minister gives out the 'notices' in church as though it didn't matter whether people responded or not. 'Take note that such and such is happening' will get exactly the result requested. People will take note. And they may well do nothing about it.

Another question is that of time-scale. Do they really want to spend the whole six months communicating, or does that time-scale include preparation time? In practice, there is an internal communication task as well as an external one: the churches to be invited to take part in the mission will need to know at least six months in advance of the mission, if not longer, so the time-scale needs revision.

Communication aims fall broadly into three categories:

◆ aims concerned with creating identity or image

◆ aims concerned with passing on information

◆ aims concerned with obtaining participation.

A communication aim is needed here that embraces all three! There needs to be an 'identity' created for the mission in the minds of the target group. Information about what is available for each section of the target group needs to be given, and it needs to be done in a way that will encourage people to take part in the appropriate parts of the mission.

Having modified the statement of aims in line with these issues, a communication aim is produced that satisfies them:

During the nine months leading up to the mission, we aim to communicate first with our members, and then with everyone living or working in the parish, in a way that creates awareness of the mission and encourages participation.

It may seem a little pedantic to spend so much time defining the obvious, but like an architect's drawing, a small inaccuracy on the plan can result in a much bigger mistake in the building!

Beware, too, of having too many aims in one plan. Here's another communication aim:

At the start of the holidays, the holiday-club leaders aim to communicate with mothers of children at the local schools, their friends and those children who go to churches nearby about the holiday club and all the activities for young people in the area so that church members will support the holiday club and provide lots of money to run it, and so that lots of children will know what we're doing.

There are a number of points here. First, the holiday-club leaders might find it easier to begin their communication programme before the start of the holidays, because they would then have access to the schools. Secondly, they need to be clear about whether they are communicating with the parents, their children, or both. Thirdly, do they really want to give out information about all the youth activities in the area? They might also find it easier to separate the aims from the tasks needed to achieve those aims. For example:

Over a three-week period, we aim to provide information about the holiday club to families in the area who have children aged between five and eleven, and to our church members in order to gain their support.

So far, so good. But things can get a bit complicated when more than two people sit down to define a communication plan. It sometimes happens that a group of people have pet projects, enthusiasms and a whole range of ideas about what needs to be done, and if the leader is more concerned with finding a place for everyone's ideas, rather than identifying a clear communication strategy, the aims can multiply so fast that the end result is unworkable.

We aim to create a clear identity for our church, communicate with parents about the work of the Sunday School, and stimulate interest in the church for the social programme so that people are empowered by the Holy Spirit to witness to their faith in a way that completes the fund-raising for the new choir robes!

GETTING EVERYBODY ON BOARD

One of the difficulties of working with any voluntary organization is that the aims and objectives of the leaders may not necessarily be shared by the members. It is wise to make no assumptions about how a communication aim that has been carefully defined in conversations with the church leaders or elders will be received by the members, and it is essential that the aims are owned not just by one section of the church, or by the church leaders, but by the whole church working together.

Without this ownership by all, not only might difficulties arise further on, but the effectiveness of the communication plan will be compromised.

In my experience, one of the best ways of getting agreement for a communication aim that can be supported by the whole church is to make a presentation of the communication aim and the reasons behind its definition to the members, with the leadership present but not leading the presentation. There is sometimes pressure to make that presentation to the elders, the church council or some other decision-making body. Resist it. Invite all the members, with sufficient lead time to enable busy, professional people to book space in their diaries. No one can then complain that they weren't consulted, and you will have the benefit of the widest cross-section of the church in the discussion.

Having made your presentation, listen carefully to the comments and criticisms. They will usually fall into one of the following areas:

◆ comments or questions which help the speaker understand the issues, or criticisms which stem from misunderstanding.

These need to be dealt with by going over the area of uncertainty with patience, avoiding giving the impression that the misunderstanding is the fault of the questioner.

◆ Suggestions or criticisms designed to modify or change the proposal. These may be attempts at helping to make the proposal stronger, or attempts to manipulate the proposal towards the areas for which the speaker has a specific concern.

These need to be listened to carefully, because they may need to be taken into account. They can either be accepted as clearly helpful, or offered to the group for comment. Try to avoid being getting into a position of defending the proposal strongly, but re-state any reasons why you believe the suggestion might not work, leaving the group to evaluate. After all, they have the responsibility under God for the ministry of their church and you will need them to support the communication aim once it is agreed.

- ◆ Objections or criticisms designed to stop the proposal. In these cases, try to discover the reasons behind the objection. They can be very revealing, and can sometimes help to redefine the communication aim in an extremely helpful way.

Try to leave the presentation with a communication aim that has been agreed by all those present. But don't assume that it will be communicated to the rest of the church. You will need to spend time communicating the results of the presentation to everyone who needs to be brought on board.

The importance of briefing every section of the church is underlined by this, probably apocryphal, story:

There was a company that wanted to launch a new product. They spent a great deal of money developing a new variety of the product, and identified a test area for the trial marketing exercise. They brought all the store managers in the trial area back to headquarters for an expensive conference, and spent a great deal of money on an expensive advertising campaign in the test area.

However, they forgot to brief the van drivers. After all, they weren't important, were they? When the time came for the new product to be delivered to the stores in the test area, the managers put out stocks of the new product alongside the old. The van drivers looked at the stocks, and wondered. There must be some mistake. These stores didn't have this particular product. Never had before, and no one had said anything about changing the orders. So the van drivers left the test product behind. The test was ruined, but the company learned one valuable lesson. Never forget to brief the van drivers.

PEOPLE, TIME AND MONEY

5

> **Good communication costs time, money and energy.**

> **Bad communication wastes time, money and energy.**

There are three basic resources needed to implement a communications plan. They are time, money, and the energy and skills of the people needed to execute it. These three resources are closely interrelated; for example, if a task has to be undertaken quickly, either more people or more money can be used. If there isn't enough money, then it might be possible to complete the task over a longer period, or use more people. Or if there are not enough people, then it might be possible to spend more money or more time to achieve the goal.

The good communicator will not only have agreed a communication aim; he or she will have taken time to quantify and agree the resources available. In fact, the second law of communications states:

> **Good communication needs resources that are agreed and deployed against clearly defined aims.**

TIME

Time is the first resource we're going to look at. There are several aspects of this particular resource: the time needed to achieve the communication aim effectively; the time of the person leading the project; and the time commitment of the people who will be involved. All these need clear definition, and need to be agreed in advance. The following check list will be useful:

◆ What is a realistic length of time needed to achieve the aims?

◆ How much time can you give personally to the project?

◆ How much time can the individual members of your team give?

◆ How much time do you have to prepare?

◆ Define the beginning and end of the project.

Try to work backwards from the target date to plan the time needed for a particular project. Let's take a simple communication project and see how the time plan works. In this case, it has been agreed that posters will be placed on 14 December for a two-week Christmas campaign.

31

SECTION ONE: A COMMUNICATIONS PLAN

TASK	DATE	LEAD TIME
Posters up	14 December	
Posters to paster	7 December	(one-week lead)
Posters from printer	1 December	(one-week lead)
Art work to printer	17 November	(fourteen days' print & lead)
Design agreed	12 November	(five-day lead)
Final design	7 November	(five-day lead)
Design discussion	1 November	(one-week lead)
Brief to design agency	15 October	(two-week lead)
Sites booked	10 October	
Brief discussed	8 October	(one-week lead)
Project initiated	1 October	

This is an average time chart for a voluntary group wanting to put up a poster campaign for Christmas. Both the start time and the finish time have been clearly defined. The latest start date is 1 October! Working from this kind of time chart it is fairly obvious that if someone is approached early in November to get a campaign going, they aregoing to have two choices: (a) move very quickly, or (b) refuse on the grounds of lack of time!

One option is to work within the time available. Suppose the approach is made on 14 November for a campaign to be posted on 14 December. The time boundaries might be worked out thus:

NOVEMBER	14	Project agreed
	15	Sites booked
	16	Design brief to agency
	23	Design presented
	24	Design modified
	28	Final design presented and agreed
DECEMBER	4	Artwork accepted and sent to printers
	8	Print collected and to pasters
	14	Posters up on sites

It can be done, but the cost is likely to escalate because both designers and printers are likely to charge extra to turn the work around in the short time available. In fact, this relationship between time, money and energy is a very important one.

The more complex a project, the more careful the project leader needs to be about time planning. A wall-chart can be employed, with each item having its own 'stream'. It is fairly easy to see at the start of each week what needs to be done, and whether each part of the project is on schedule. At the start of a project, a rough estimate of the time needed can, and should, be worked out so that a realistic start date can be estimated.

If it is essential to have a clear idea of when a project needs to start, it is equally important to know when the project will end. If you are asking people to give time to a project, they need to know that they won't be working on it for ever. In order to be able to make a decision, they need to know that you are asking them for a specific amount of time—one evening a week for three months, for example. In fact, one the best ways of assessing a project is to ask when it is due to be completed.

I once took part in a mission where invitation cards were an important part of the communication plan. Unfortunately, the person running this part of the plan forgot to check on the time it would take to print and deliver the cards. They arrived at the mission office only twenty-four hours before the event they were to be used for. Not only did the event itself misfire, but the cost of the printing and the work of the volunteer were both wasted.

> **Good time planning uses resources wisely.**

> **Poor time planning wastes resources.**

Time-keeping is an important task for one of the members of the team. Usually it is the leader who takes this on, but in a complex project it might be advisable to appoint one person whose sole job is to manage the time planning. Bringing the project in on time is usually one of the most important success factors.

MONEY

Money is the second resource we're going to look at. There are two basic approaches to running the finances of any communication task. The first is to be given a budget by the organizing committee, and in my experience, this is how most church projects work. The organizing committee, in planning an event or a year's activities, set aside a specific sum, often, in the communicator's view, quite inadequate for the task, and ask for an impossible amount of work to be done within the offered budget. The aspiring communicator has three choices: (a) to accept the challenge and do their best; (b) to demonstrate the inadequacy of the budget and seek an increase; (c) to refuse the challenge.

The other approach, which is far less common, is for the communicator to be asked to present a communication plan and an associated budget. This is by far the most professional approach, as it gives the communicator the opportunity not only to argue a financial case, but to discuss with the organizing committee a range of options, and to get a very early agreement to a communications plan.

Both approaches are attempts to balance two things: what is a realistic budget for the funding group to provide, and what is realistic for the needs of the communicator.

There are, however, ways of increasing an inadequate budget, provided that the funding group agrees. It is possible for the communicator to include on the team someone whose role is to raise an agreed sum to supplement the budget. This can be done either by direct fund-raising, or by seeking sponsorship for specific items. Printed programmes, for example, can sometimes attract sponsorship from local or even national traders. It is also possible to approach individuals who are known to support specific areas of mission. There may be local trust funds that can be approached for grant aid.

Whichever approach is used, it is very important that the budget is agreed both personally and structurally. By this, I mean that the members of the funding organization need personally to own the amount of money that is being spent (after all, it is likely that they are going to be asked to give it), and the appropriate structural authority needs to be obtained.

One way of helping a funding group to put a budget into perspective is to try to analyse what the group currently spends on their communications. Most voluntary organizations, if asked, will say that they don't spend a great deal on communications. Yet if a list is made, it can be very revealing. How much, for example, is hidden in 'stationary costs'? In photocopying or duplication? How much is spent on telephone calls or on magazine costs?

In any communication task where an annual plan is proposed, it can be very helpful to try to identify how much was spent in the previous year on communications. Remembering the maxim that 'bad communication wastes time, money and energy', it can be very revealing to identify costs over a previous twelve-month period against results achieved, and compare it with the proposed plan.

However, at the beginning of a project, it is likely that only an outline budget can be either presented or approved. I tend to err on the side of caution in defining an outline budget. I usually take the highest optimum figure for costs, and where income is concerned, I take a low view. That way, all the surprises are usually nice ones! Once an outline budget is presented, and the broad task agreed, it is possible either to spend time on refining the budget proposal, or to give the task to one of the team. Here, people work in different ways. My own preference is to keep tight personal control on costs, and so the refining of the budget is something that I either do myself, or take close personal interest in.

Budgets are never a statement of what will happen: they are guidelines of what must not be exceeded. It is the mark of a good communicator that changes in the projected figures are recognized as they happen, communicated to the team, and reflected in reports to the organizing committee. If you can develop a culture of good stewardship within the team that you will have to build for any major project, it will help you to do more with the resources you have been given.

The final skill is to bring the project in on, or marginally under, budget. It's not a matter of saying, 'If I don't spend it all, I won't get so much next time.' Rather, it's a matter of being a good steward, and making the limited resources you have been given work as hard for the kingdom of God as they can (see the parable of the talents!). The key to this skill is in getting quotations for every serious item of expenditure, not making 'spur of the moment' buying decisions, but sticking like glue to your communications plan, and in using all the skills and resources that are offered to you free or at low cost.

People will inevitably come to you with a 'good idea' which happens to cost money. It might be an excellent idea, and a good communicator listens to them all, and evaluates them all in the light of the communication aim and plan. But they only get implemented if (a) they fit the communications plan, and (b) they are sufficiently high on the priority list to take up the bit of slack in the budget that was won from getting a better-than-expected quotation in another area. In my experience, it's when people get carried away by enthusiasm for a good idea when there is no money available, that things start to go wrong.

Even in the best-organized projects, it sometimes happens that the costs begin to escalate beyond the budget projections. The important thing to remember if this happens to you is that it is your responsibility to share the problem with the organizing committee, or its chairperson. Don't just wait for the problem to go away: it will probably get worse. If you are making regular reports to the organizing committee, or the person or people who have authorized the project, then you will be in a position to bring to their attention the facts and the reasons. Not only have you shared the difficulty, but you will have acted responsibly with other people's money. And with discussion, it is possible to agree a revised budget, or a revised communications plan, that puts things on the right track again.

HUMAN RESOURCES

We're now talking about people, and people bring three things to a communication project: energy, skills and insight. First, there is simply a wealth of things to do, and the competent communicator recognizes that he or she cannot do everything personally. In almost every communications plan there is the need for a team. Let's use as an example the communication aim we defined earlier:

During the six months leading up to the mission, we aim to communicate with everyone living or working in the parish in a way that creates awareness of the mission and encourages them to take part.

The communications plan is likely to call for several major areas of work. These can be roughly assessed from the statement of aim, and may well include the following: internal communications, for managing the communication with church members; design and print buying, for managing the design and printing of posters, leaflets, brochures etc.; press and media relations, for promoting the event in the local and regional press, radio and television; events co-ordination, to work with the people who are producing the brochures and posters, to ensure that dates are correct and events don't get missed; and copywriting and advertising, to ensure that brochures and leaflets are written properly, and that advertising is bought cost-effectively where needed. To this might be added a visitor team to manage the task of visiting all the organizations and groups in the parish with information about the mission, with its coordinator as a member of the communication team. A six-member team, with a coordinating team leader, will provide an ideal resource base to bring the communication plan to completion.

However, it is unlikely that any individual congregation is going to have experienced and professional designers, media buyers, press relations officers and copywriters in one congregation. So the task for the team leader is either to locate these skills within the community, or 'borrow' them from other churches, or to appoint people to the team who are capable either of drawing on the experience of others or of learning very quickly!

It is always possible to recruit help on a 'consultancy' basis. In most denominations there is someone responsible for communications who will know people who are working in the various communication professions, and who might be available to act as consultants to the team member responsible for that particular skill, or who might give advice and direction to the team. This makes very effective use of the skills of the consultant, who is relieved of having to do the 'donkey work', and also gives to the team member a valuable set of lessons on how to do the job.

Running a communication team is a skill in itself, and there are several things that help a team to work effectively:

◆ Everyone should have a clear idea of the communications plan and what the desired end result will be.

◆ Everyone should have a clear idea about the job they are being asked to do—and what they are not being asked to do—together with any delegated budget you might give them.

◆ There should be regular meetings of the team. There is nothing more dangerous than meeting only when problems occur—the team members end up feeling stressed and undervalued. Equally, it is not wise to limit meetings to 'opportunities'. Regular meetings allow the team to gel, to settle role and boundary problems with their own tasks, and to keep each other motivated towards the goal.

◆ Difficulties should always be faced. Burying them, or putting them off until later, usually results in them getting worse.

Where a team exists, it is important that the team both owns the communications plan, and has accepted the plan as a logical outworking of the communication aim. This is particularly true where professional communicators are members of the team. It can be helpful to spend the first meeting, and possibly the second, going through the communication aim, and getting individual team members to comment on the suggested plan. Quite often it can be considerably improved from the comments and suggestions of the team. Not only that, but the team then feels involved in the whole plan, and it often helps them to clarify their role and tasks within the team.

Using your resources wisely and effectively is the key to getting the results you need. It can be both challenging and great fun to see how far you can take a project on a limited, and often inadequate, budget.

IDENTIFYING THOSE YOU WANT TO REACH 6

So far we have collected data and defined a communication aim. An outline budget has been prepared, a team has been identified and a time-scale set. The next task is to sit down with the team and get a clear picture of the various groups of people that we want to communicate with. This is where the plan really begins to take shape, because we're getting to the point at which we're identifying who we want to reach, and beginning to formulate ideas about how we might want to reach them. Identifying the various 'target groups' is often done best by 'brainstorming', because by doing it this way we're less likely to miss important groups of people. Let's take a couple of the communication aims we defined earlier and look at how they might be targeted:

During the nine months leading up to the mission, we aim to communicate first with our members, and then with everyone living or working in the parish, in a way that creates awareness of the mission and encourages participation.

The first, and most obvious boundary is geographical—everyone living or working in the parish—so the team might find it helpful to start with a map detailed enough to show all the areas of the parish, with roads and any other important details.

The next three divisions are again relatively straightforward: first, church members; secondly, people living in the parish; and thirdly, people working but not necessarily living in the parish.

The next step is probably to look at the draft programme for the mission. The purpose of breaking down the groups further is to be able to link them with information about the mission that might be particularly appropriate to them. The draft programme shows events suitable for parents and toddlers, children, young people aged 11–15, young adults, a 'parents' workshop', retired people's meetings, business lunches and a major rally for all ages.

The access points for each of these groups, using the map and the local knowledge of the team, are identified as follows:

SECTION ONE: A COMMUNICATIONS PLAN

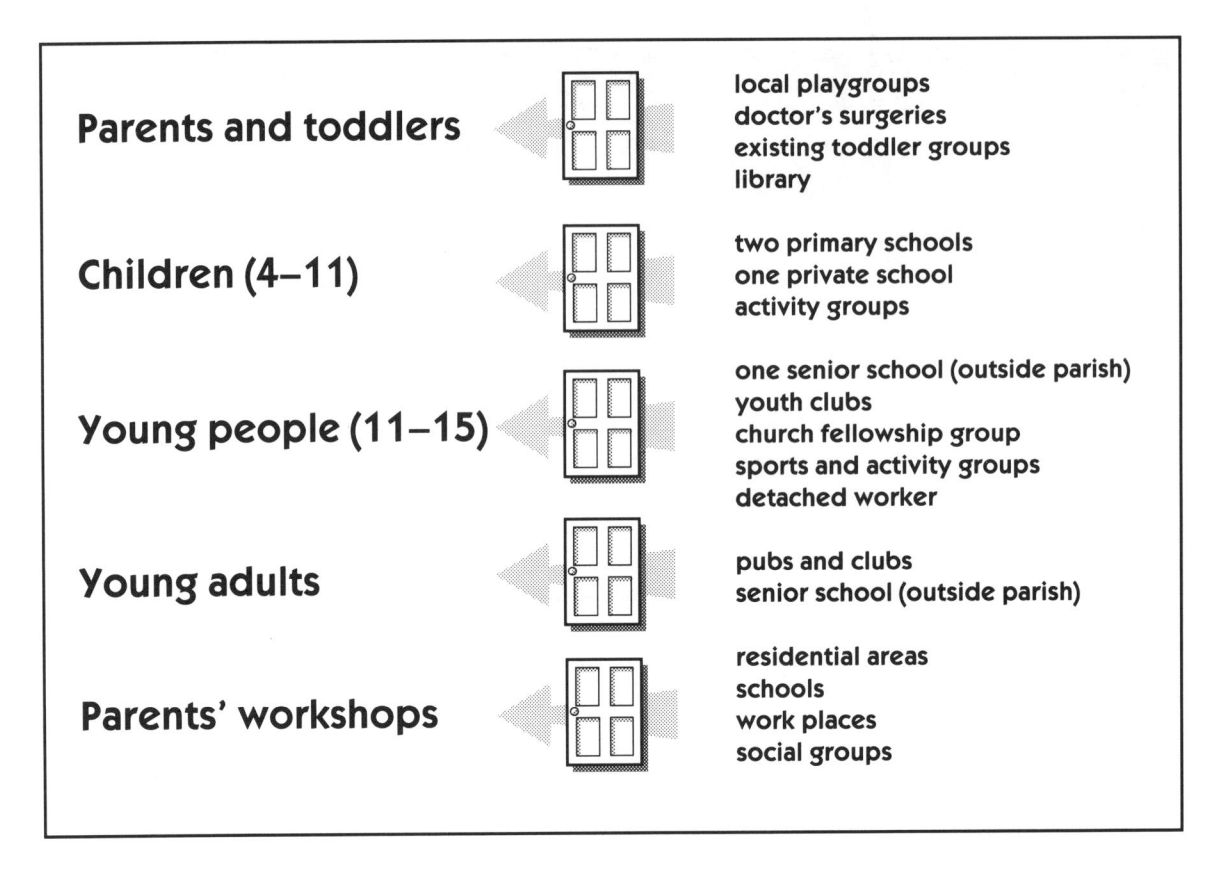

Group	Contact points
Parents and toddlers	local playgroups doctor's surgeries existing toddler groups library
Children (4–11)	two primary schools one private school activity groups
Young people (11–15)	one senior school (outside parish) youth clubs church fellowship group sports and activity groups detached worker
Young adults	pubs and clubs senior school (outside parish)
Parents' workshops	residential areas schools work places social groups

The list could go on. The point of the exercise is to have a clear picture of the various groups of people that need to be addressed by the communications plan, and to have some idea of the points at which they can be contacted.

So far, the listing has been about the details: creating discrete groups of people who might be addressed by one form of medium or another. But there is another part of the communication aim which needs to be addressed, so that an awareness of the mission is created.

Creating an overall awareness is as important as making sure that all the groups which need to be contacted are listed. This can be done in several ways. First, and perhaps most obvious, is the creation of an 'identity' for the mission by the use of colours, images, a logo, and so on. The project has a 'personality', created in part by the nature of the event itself, and in part by the approach the communication team takes towards the event. Sometimes, this 'personality' depends on the market research, the 'data', that has already been collected.

For example, in creating a 'personality' for a new radio station, the programme director commissioned some market research which showed that the station needed to be a warm, female professional, with high intelligence and a broad interest in current affairs, but with a love of popular chart music. This 'personality' was reflected in everything from the name of the station, through its advertising and presentation, to the programmes and presenters. Because the 'personality' of the station matched that which was expected by the potential audience, it was a success from day one.

We will look in detail at creating an overall 'feel' to the project in Chapter 9, when we look at defining the message. But for now, it is important simply to remember that our list of people, or groups of people, need to be held together as part of a whole: that although we have identified specific groups of people to be addressed by different parts of our communications plan, they need to be held together as potential participants in one creative event.

So far, we have looked at targeting in terms of a mission, a specific event which has a beginning and an end. But the same processes apply to the management of the day-to-day communications plan for a congregation, or a church fellowship. Internal communications need the same treatment, and even when a church is simply going about its day-to-day work of teaching, pastoring and visiting, it needs to be sure that nobody is being missed out.

Structuring the list of people you want to reach, and incorporating them into the communications plan, is the key to ensuring that the time, money and energy you are putting in is kept focused on the groups of people you need to reach. It can help to check out the list with the organizing committee in one of the regular reports that are going to be made to them—it will help keep you focused as well!

7 WHAT RESPONSE DO YOU WANT?

It's one of the common, yet puzzling aspects of church communication that we spend hundreds of hours and large sums of money communicating with people without any clear idea about what we want them to do as a result! All too often we treat our communication as though we were broadcasting information, rather than challenging people to make a decision. We use the 'take note' approach, rather than giving people a clear indication of what we want them to do as a result.

How often do we hear the minister complain: 'I don't know why I give out the notices in church—no one seems to listen.' There may be many reasons why the 'notices' get forgotten. It might be because people are trying to concentrate on other things at the time (such as the act of worship they have come to engage in), or simply that they physically cannot hear. But more often it's because the person communicating does so in a way that does not create reaction or invite response. A notice saying, 'The church fête is on 28 June,' could all too easily get the response, 'Thanks for warning me!', whereas a notice which says 'We need a good turnout for the fête on 28 June, so I would like you to mark the date in your diary, and make every effort to come along' at least makes clear what is wanted.

There is a marvellous story about the minister who was fed up with giving out a fundraising notice to which no one responded. So he decided to be very specific about the response he wanted. He stood up the following Sunday and said: 'I want everyone here this morning to take out their wallets, open them, and say after me: "Help yourself"!'

Response is one of the clearest of the gospel criteria. Jesus came into Galilee saying: 'Repent, and believe the gospel.' This was a straightforward declaration of the two responses he wanted from his hearers.

The great open-air evangelists also make a point about being clear about the response they hope to provoke. 'If you want to commit yourself to following Jesus tonight, I want you to get up out of your seat and to come down to the front where someone will pray with you.' Whatever you make of the theology behind the call, the call itself is quite clear. The response is spelled out, and no one can be in any doubt about what is wanted.

Being clear about the desired response also helps to avoid the dishonesty of manipulation. Manipulation happens when the result is hidden, rather than openly stated; when we try to get people to do things we want them to do without making the choices clear. One form of manipulation that used to be common in some circles was the ubiquitous 'survey'. It wasn't a proper data-gathering exercise at all; rather, it was a subterfuge to get people talking about their faith. People would visit door-to-door with a clipboard, and would ask if the respondent minded answering a few questions 'for a survey we're doing'. Frankly, it was a lie. What was being done was an attempt at evangelism, because the questions were intended not to gather data, but to evoke a discussion leading the person towards Christian commitment. Thankfully, this rather blatant form of manipulation is much less common than it used to be.

There are other forms of manipulation which are far more subtle, and the only way to be sure that your own communication is not contaminated by hidden manipulation is by asking the question, 'What response is required?' and then making sure that the choices are clear and open.

The third law of communication states:

> **Being open about the desired response empowers people to choose and to change.**

> **Hiding the desired response in a manipulative way destroys freedom of choice and restricts change.**

Giving people the freedom to choose by making a clear statement about the response you want may limit the number of responses you get, but it is much closer to the gospel criteria of open communication, and the responses will be of much higher quality. After all, the cross itself is the most open choice of all—and probably the most difficult. The open challenge of the cross is one of the distinctive marks of the gospel. It is also part of the cost of discipleship that not everyone accepts the challenge of the cross.

So it will be with any communication that is based on Christian principles. The cost of openness about the desired result will be rejection, both of the message and also possibly of the messenger. People rarely have the ability to distinguish between the two. We become 'representative' people, indistinguishable from the message we are carrying.

So far, we have designed the framework for a communications plan which has been based on collected data, has a clear aim, a clear budget of time and resources, is clear about the groups of people it is trying to reach, and has an open and defined set of responses. We can define the desired responses in a way that helps us to measure our success in communicating. For example, let's take the communication aim we defined earlier:

During the nine months leading up to the mission, we aim to communicate first with our members, and then with everyone living or working in the parish, in a way that creates awareness of the mission and encourages participation.

We have already broken this down into specific target groups. One of these is the family with children under the age of four. We can define the response we want from this group fairly clearly:

We want all parents with families under the age of four to know about the mission activities suitable for their children, and to bring them along to those activities.

Two desired responses, then:

◆ knowledge of the events

◆ participation in the events.

We can focus our desired results even more sharply. We want the parents to both know and feel good about the mission activities, and we want them to come to a specific address at a specific time for a specific number of days.

Let's look at another example, this time of a slightly more complex communication aim. The task is to improve the image of a local congregation, and the time-scale that the communication team have taken is one year. The data they have collected tells them that the image of the congregation held by people living in the surrounding area is very different from the reality that members of the congregation themselves experience. Words like 'musty', 'dull', 'old-fashioned', and 'out-of-date' occur over and over again in the data collected from local residents. The communication aim is then defined as follows:

Over a twelve-month period we aim to improve the image of our church in the perception of those people resident in our catchment area so that they are more attracted to the work of Christ in their midst.

It is a reasonable aim, and the resources have been quantified. A group of five people will spend no more than five hours each a week developing and executing a plan to achieve the aim, with a budget of no more than one tenth of the church's income.

The key influences, those people or things which help define 'image', have been identified and targeted. They include the church building itself (which gives an feeling of disrepair and neglect), the posters and notices on the notice-board, the paper communication from the church, the local newspaper (which has carried hardly any stories which present the church in a fresh and vital way), and the congregation's involvement in the local community (or lack of it).

Clearly, there are issues here that are the proper concern of a communications plan, and issues that can only be dealt with by the church members themselves. And this highlights a very important feature of the role of the communicator: he or she needs a two-way relationship with the church or organization. It is a waste of a professional communicator, as well as being thoroughly demoralizing, simply to treat him or her as a means of 'getting the message across'. The communicator can tell you very quickly where there are problems with the organization or church that is trying to communicate, and is often hamstrung by faults or failings that could easily be put right; but it is a rare and satisfying organization that is prepared to listen!

MEASURING THE RESULTS 8

The whole point of spending time constructing a communications plan is to get a specific and predetermined result. It might be to inform people, or to get their participation, or to improve the image of a church or group. It's good to spend time and money on implementing a communications plan, but unless it contains some way of measuring the result, there's no objective way of telling whether the plan is achieving its aims or not.

There are other reasons why it's important to measure success or failure. Perhaps most important is the responsibility of being good stewards of the time, money and energy that people are contributing. If, say, a monthly newsletter aimed at informing young people about youth events is not being read, it's not much use continuing, month after month, to produce it. It's wasting time, paper, money, and probably someone's energy. Better to find out what is going wrong, and make some changes. Equally, if a large amount of money is being spent on newspaper advertisements, and there is little return from the readers, it's probably sensible to use the money in other ways.

Perhaps equally important is the need to use effective measurement to prevent the communicator assuming inappropriate personal blame. The results of a particular communications plan may not be immediately apparent, and even the most experienced communicator can be left wondering whether it's been worthwhile. If some method can be found to measure the results, this removes any possible element of personal doubt, and frees the communicator either to report a clearly demonstrable success, or to find out why the plan is failing to achieve its aims, and to correct it.

And then there is the need, if the plan really is failing to achieve its objective, of learning from the experience, and finding ways of putting things right. How often have we heard the words, 'We tried it once and it didn't work.' How do you know it didn't work? Why didn't it work? What needed to be done to make it work? Unless a way of measuring can be found, a quiet success might in time become the tyranny of an assumed failure.

There are very few things that are not capable of measurement in some form or other, and communication is no exception. The next law of communication states:

The success or failure of a communications plan is measured by the results it achieves.

43

In other words, to find out how to measure the success or failure of a particular communications plan, we can look at the desired results and find a way of comparing them with the actual results. Once again, let's take one of the aims we defined earlier, and see how the responses might be measured:

During the nine months leading up to the mission, we aim to communicate first with our members, and then with everyone living or working in the parish, in a way that creates awareness of the mission and encourages participation.

There are two obvious results required from this aim: awareness and participation. Clearly, the ability of the plan to create awareness in the target groups is going to affect the level of participation, so this is the first measure that is defined. There are also two groups of people who need to be aware of the mission: the church members themselves (measuring the effectiveness of the internal communication), and those people they are trying to reach (measuring the effectiveness of the external communication).

What level of awareness itself constitutes success is more a matter of personal or team choice. Though it might be reasonable to choose a figure at or near to 100 per cent awareness for church members, particularly when there is only one church involved, it would be unrealistic to expect to achieve anywhere near 100 per cent awareness from the external plan. After discussion, the team decide that success will be achieved if:

◆ ninety-eight per cent of church members are aware of the mission two months before launch

◆ sixty per cent of everyone living or working in the parish are aware of the mission one week before the launch.

It can be fascinating, and very motivating for the team, to measure in a way that shows the awareness building up. For example, a simple poll of the congregation at the beginning of the nine-month period, repeated at intervals of one month, should show a steeply rising graph. Another simple poll of a representative sample of the local population should also show a rising graph, and there might be peaks after particular promotional events. It can be useful if one member of the communication team has responsibility for managing the samples, and for reporting to the team each month.

The simple poll can be broken down further, by asking other questions designed to show which of the targeted groups the respondents belong to. This way, much more detailed information can be fed back to the team, and specific gaps in the profile can be spotted and dealt with as the plan progresses. For example, the report after seven months might show that the following percentages of those groups polled were aware of the mission logo and its meaning:

church members	100%
parents with toddlers	29%
young people 11–16	2%
young adults	0%
local businesses	14%

A similar report after eight months might show the following figures:

church members *(a new family had just joined, and all four members were unaware of the mission)*	80%
parents with toddlers	58%
young people 11–16	22%
young adults	12%
local businesses	19%

This result showed the team that the part of their plan aimed at young adults was not achieving the desired result, and they were able to revise the plan to concentrate on this particular target group.

This simple way of measuring awareness can be built into the plan, and executed throughout the nine months of its duration. But the measurement of participation presents slightly more of a problem. It would be counter-productive to the mission to have someone standing at the door of the various events asking people questions as they came in. One way is to have someone quietly count all the known church members, and subtract them from total attendance. Another is for a response card to be produced which has a tick box for first-time attendance. The team will probably be able to find appropriate ways of measuring that will not be unduly intrusive.

A quantitative survey of a representative sample can be an excellent way of measuring, but whilst this can sometimes be done easily (knocking at twenty doors in an area), there are other times when it is not so easy. One method of informal measurement is to chat casually to a number of people, introducing the thing to be measured into the conversation. To help in counting, one finger curled on the right hand is a positive response, one finger curled on the left hand is a negative response. It's not the most accurate method, but it is sometimes the only way to find out what we need to know.

Whatever method you decide to use, it is important that this aspect of the communication plan does not get lost in the heat of execution. Although it might seem an irritation, or even a diversion of energy before the plan is executed, it will be even more frustrating afterwards if there is no objective measurement by which success or failure can be determined.

CHOOSING THE MEDIA 9

The next step is to decide how we are going to reach the groups of people we have identified. Technically, the means of carrying the message is called the medium, and where we use more than one, the media. The common understanding of the word 'media' refers mainly to television, radio and newspapers, but there are many more forms of media, and all of them are potential means of communication.

Although we will by now have a good idea of the kind of messages we want to get across to our 'target' groups, the precise form they will take will depend on the media choices we make. But here, things get a little complicated, because, as the saying goes, 'the medium is the message', or at least, the media we choose can themselves convey a message about us. A church which chooses to use a heavy advertising programme on the local radio station and in newspapers, coupled with free distribution leaflets, is going to convey a different message about itself from the church which has chosen only to use the members of their Christian community to communicate with people on a one-to-one basis.

The choice of media is as much an art as a science, and individual choices will differ. For this very reason it is important that, once the communication plan has been completed and the media choices listed and costed, it needs to be both agreed and owned by the local church or churches involved. It's no use putting together what you think is an exciting plan which uses a high level of advertising if the culture of the church is focused towards a 'human community' style of communication.

There are two basic approaches to choosing appropriate media. The first is to use existing media, and more specifically, media that are already part of the culture of the selected or 'target' groups. The second is to create your own media, and introduce them to the 'target' group.

Examples of existing media (which we will look at in detail in Section Two) are:

◆ newspapers—tabloid, broadsheet, free & trade

◆ radio—community, local, regional & national

◆ television—cable, terrestrial & satellite

◆ magazines

◆ the telephone

◆ the individual

◆ notice-boards

◆ church notices

◆ networks and newsletters

◆ local information points, such as libraries, tourist information points, local directories, etc.

Examples of specially created media (again covered in detail in Section Two) are:

- posters—from A4 up to billboard size
- leaflets
- direct mailing
- car stickers and 'gimmick' items
- own newspapers
- special-event radio
- competitions and free offers.

There is a third option, which is to pay for advertising space in existing media. It is 'created' in the sense that the pictures and messages carried in the space you have bought are (subject to regulations) created by you and under your control, but 'existing' in the sense that they are carried in existing media, whether printed or broadcast.

It is unlikely that any single medium will be sufficient to meet the communication aim. Almost certainly there will need to be a range of different media, reinforcing each other but together achieving the required results. Using existing media for any particular 'target group' requires an understanding of that group: whether there is a common medium that members of that group all read, and where they normally get their information from.

For example, if we were intending to communicate with a group of local sports fishermen, the following existing media might be available:

- a local fishing club newsletter
- the specialist fishing magazines
- a fishing or sports programme on local radio
- individual members of the fishing club
- the fishing column in the local newspaper
- the fishing or sports correspondents of local or regional radio or television
- the local fishing tackle shop.

In addition, it might be necessary to produce some of our own media to supplement the use of existing media. Posters or leaflets with a picture of a sports fisherman landing a good fish and carrying the message we want to give might attract members of our target group, as might a competition showing a prize of fishing tackle. Using particular visual images to attract members of the 'target group' are discussed in Chapter 19.

Its not always possible to know what media might be suitable for a particular 'target group', and again some research will be needed. Most media-conscious countries (which in today's world means most countries) have commercial publications which list the various media under special-interest categories, and usually include the specialist correspondents for newspaper, radio and television as well. Any public relations practitioner will be able to list the best of these publications, although they are usually provided on a subscription-only basis and can be expensive.

Another, and easier, way of finding out what media might be appropriate to your target group is simply to chat to one or two members of that group. Try to find out what they read, where they get their information, and if there is any common information link (such as a newsletter or club) that they belong to. Then start drawing up your media profile.

It can also be helpful, at the start of a

project, to build a media list which covers the major newspapers, radio and television outlets in the area, together with any specialist correspondents who will need to be kept informed. The list can be both geographical, covering the major general media outlets in a particular area, and specialist, listing those media which cover the interests of the particular target groups. List the media, with their editors' and news editors' telephone and fax numbers; include any personal contacts who might need to be kept informed; and have a section for 'internal media', such as the name, address and telephone number of the parish magazine editors, religious newspapers, etc.

Most professional communicators have a 'contacts' book, in which they record the names, addresses and telephone/fax numbers of people they have made contact with over the years. Some journalists are even recruited on the basis that the people in their contacts book will be most useful to the publication, and it can be a great help to the local church communicator to do the same in reverse, as it were.

Let's take one of the target groups from the following project:

During the nine months leading up to the mission, we aim to communicate first with our members, and then with everyone living or working in the parish, in a way that creates awareness of the mission and encourages participation.

The culture of this particular target group is a high level of listening to the local independent radio station, interaction with friends, video hire, with a high attendance at clubs and activities.

Therefore the media choice consists of:

◆ advertisements on the ILR station

◆ posters in schools, clubs, video shops, etc.

◆ personal briefing of key leaders (detached youth worker, club leaders, etc.)

◆ free tickets to the youth events.

The target group we choose as an example is:

Young people (11–15) ⬅ one senior school (outside parish):
youth clubs
church fellowship group
sports and activity groups
detached worker

In addition, a well-known Christian sports personality could be asked to endorse the events (including the radio advertisement), and to speak at the youth events themselves.

There is a value-added bonus to taking advertising on the ILR station. The newsroom is alerted to the event, and a reasonable amount of coverage is gained.

Another way of reaching people is to use direct mail. Professional people tend to dismiss so-called 'junk mail' as intrusive, and will tend not to use it. That's because they are used to getting letters, and usually find dealing with the mail is a chore, rather than a pleasure. But for some groups of people, letters are unusual, and give a great deal of pleasure. They are something out of the ordinary, and can be very useful for gaining attention. Direct mail can:

◆ convey specific information to carefully targeted audiences

◆ provide a useful response mechanism

◆ reinforce a sense of belonging.

Direct mail is particularly useful in keeping members of an organization aware that they are still members. Simply by sending a letter every six months, the first message received is: 'You still belong.' If, as well as strengthening the sense of belonging, the mailshot can educate, or raise extra funds, it will have achieved a great deal. I have often wondered why the churches don't use direct mail. It fits exactly the criteria that so many churches struggle with: dispersed members who are vaguely aware of their membership, yet who might be persuaded into more active forms of belonging by a gentle reminder. It can also be a very personal form of communication if used on a local scale. The vicar or minister of a parish can write personally to each and every resident, and for special events (*not* merely for fundraising) the impact can be considerable.

Churches may not use this means of communication because the one thing needed for a direct mailshot is missing from the churches: a selective address list. These are often built commercially from competitions. Competitions are designed to attract people who form a potential market, and the entries are entered onto a computerized address list which is then used for targeted marketing, which is why those people who enter a lot of competitions often find themselves the target of large amounts of direct mail! It can also appear to be expensive in terms of postage or distribution. However, the cost of postage needs to be weighed against the very real advantage of communicating directly with a very large number of people. Break down the cost of the mailshot into the cost of contacting each individual. Done like this, it can appear to be a very cost-effective way of communicating.

Direct mail can also provide a mechanism for response. A freepost licence is usually fairly cheap, and only those letters which are returned are charged to the account. So every postage stamp paid for is a return that can be followed up. I know of one church which used a freepost reply coupon on every edition of their newsletter. They advertised a free booklet on the Christian faith, and over the years they found a regular trickle of enquirers.

Whatever your final media choices are, they should suit the target audience, and be chosen to reflect the nature of the originator. Think creatively, be imaginative, and be prepared to reject choices that don't seem to fit the image of the church you are working with.

DEFINING THE MESSAGE 10

Having chosen the most suitable media, now is the time to define the message. Remember the key issues:

◆ What response do you want?

◆ Who are you talking to?

◆ What medium are you using?

◆ Can you use pictures as well as words?

WHAT RESPONSE DO YOU WANT?

The message should clearly indicate the desired response. For example:

> **COME TO THE Children's Service**
> at
> St Mark's on Sunday
> 10.30 am
> ... and bring a friend!

The message is clear, because the desired response is well-defined. A particularly striking message used in England recently came from a Christmas advertising campaign used by a number of churches:

> GIVE JESUS A BIRTHDAY PRESENT.
> WRAP UP THE KIDS AND BRING THEM TO CHURCH.
>
> †
>
> REMEMBER WHAT IT'S ALL ABOUT.
> COME TO CHURCH THIS CHRISTMAS.

There are a number of messages operating here. The first conveys a message about Christmas itself. Whatever else Christmas might be, it is a celebration of Jesus' birthday. The second message requires a response. It's a clever message not only because of the play on words between 'presents' and 'wrapping up'—both evocative of nice things—but also because many English churches are chilly places in winter, and it's something of a traditional family activity to put on woolly hats and scarves and go out together to church. This message was designed by a professional advertising agency, and it shows!

WHO ARE YOU TALKING TO?

The message you define will depend as much on the person or people you want to talk to as on what you want to say. It's a useful exercise to compare two newspapers: one aimed at the financial leaders of a country, and the other at manual labourers. The first will probably be characterized by the following:

◆ complex, technical language

◆ few pictures

◆ small print

◆ longer words and sentences

◆ longer, more complex stories.

The second, however, is likely to be quite different:

◆ simple, straightforward language

◆ large pictures, and plenty of them

◆ larger print

◆ simple vocabulary, short sentences

◆ short stories.

There is likely to be one other difference: in the newspaper aimed at financial leaders, the editor will adopt a style that reports the facts and allows the reader to make up his or her mind about the implications. With the newspaper aimed at manual workers, the editor is much more likely to 'lead' his or her readers: to tell them what to think or how to feel about an issue by subtle use of pictures or words.

I'm not suggesting that the church should be manipulative in any of its communication: what is important is that it should recognize who is being addressed, and define the message in suitable language. Take the following wording on a Church notice board as an example:

Sung matins
at 11.00 am

Choral evensong
at 6.30 pm

What kind of person is likely to respond? Clearly, the message appeals to those 'in the know', the lovers of matins or evensong. Matins is a 'club' word: it describes an activity which will appeal to a particular brand of church member. But for most people who don't go to church, matins is a curious or even meaningless word. The message is clear: If you're not 'one of us', you'll feel excluded.

Compare the following:

Family worship
at 11 am

Evening worship
and discussion groups
7.30 pm

Here the message has changed. No longer is the reader baffled by 'club' words like 'matins' or 'evensong', but is faced with the much more open word 'family'. The addition of the 'discussion groups' gives another message: 'We expect you to take part.' The disadvantages are that not everyone feels that they belong to a family, and certainly not everyone wants to participate in a discussion which could expose their own ignorance or vulnerability.

Beware of messages which contain 'club' words or convey 'club' meanings. If the message is designed to reinforce your own distinctive identity amongst the community of Christians, that's fine. But if the aim is to reach those outside the church, 'club' words almost always convey exclusion. Try making a list a 'club' words to avoid.

USING PICTURES

Pictures are as important as words in the content of the message, and can be particularly useful in conveying feelings.

The message 'Remember the people of Somalia' is not, by itself, particularly striking. But put it below a picture of starving children, and add a response coupon for donations, and there is a powerful message operating at several levels.

Pictures can be used either as the main message, or as a hook to draw people's attention to the main message. Here is a profile of one particular target group:

Age: 12–14 years old
Main interest: mountain bikes
Desired response: to come on a mountain bike weekend
Medium: poster

MOUNTAIN BIKE WEEKEND

28 Feb 2000
at St John's
St John's Road
Anytown

St John's
Reaching out into the community

Please bring your helmet.

The poster picture could well feature a group of friendly young teenagers holding their mountain bikes with a tent in the background. The picture is a hook—it attracts those with a particular interest in mountain bikes, and tells a story. The words on the poster could read:

You could join them next weekend. For details... etc.

CHOOSE A MESSAGE THAT SUITS YOUR CHOSEN MEDIUM

If you have chosen to use posters, then the number of words you can use will be very limited. You might be able to convey more by the picture on the poster than by the words themselves. But if you have chosen a newspaper, then you can usually say a great deal more in words.

Remember:

◆ think in pictures as well as words

◆ use pictures to convey feelings

◆ choose words that will suit your chosen audience

◆ avoid 'club' words unless you are addressing members

◆ define your message according to the medium you have chosen.

THE IMPORTANCE OF TESTING

One of the most important things you can do, once you have defined your message, is to try it out on a member of the target audience. This testing can vary from a quick check with a friend to a full-scale research programme. Pre-testing your communication has several advantages:

◆ it ensures that what you're saying is what you want to say

◆ it makes sure that there are no secondary messages that you have failed to spot

◆ it gives a sample of how your message is likely to be received

The Christian relief agency, Christian Aid, tested a major advertising campaign. They had taken the theme 'empowering the poor', and wanted to develop a campaign around the theme. But when they tested it, they discovered that very few people understood what was meant by 'empowering the poor'. Their agency suggested a different phrase: 'We believe in life before death.' It remains one of the more successful Christian campaign themes.

You don't need the high cost of a formal research programme if you're a small church or organization. A simple test can easily be set up. Invite a few people to someone's home. They should be people drawn from a similar background to the people you are trying to reach. Then show them your communication material. Let them give their feelings and reactions to your design. Ask what their response would be to the communication if they saw it used.

Listen to any suggestions they make for improving it. Then, when they have gone home, spend some time reflecting on what you have heard and see if any changes are needed.

Sometimes, the final choice of message can challenge your initial choice of media. Suppose, for example, that you have budgeted for posters as the main medium in a campaign. But when you have defined the final message, you need more words than can possibly be put on a simple poster. One way out may well be to change the media choice.

One other thing needs to be said about defining the message. It is simply that the most powerful message of all is how we live our lives as Christians. No matter how carefully we define particular messages, they can be drowned out by inappropriate behaviour. Remember the maxim: 'What you are doing is shouting so loudly that I can't hear what you're saying'.

11 EXECUTING THE PLAN

If you have followed the steps outlined in the previous chapters you will have:

◆ obtained approval and permission to construct a plan

◆ carefully defined and agreed your aims

◆ defined and agreed your budget and resources

◆ identified those you want to reach

◆ agreed the desired responses

◆ decided on what will make your plan a success

◆ decided who the message will come from

◆ chosen the appropriate media

◆ defined the message.

■ USE YOUR TEAM

By now, you are likely to have gathered around you a small team of people, each with specific tasks, working together to achieve the aim. Now, more than at any time, there need to be regular meetings of the team programmed into the diary. The task of the team is:

◆ to complete individual tasks

◆ to co-ordinate individual tasks into one plan

◆ to support each other

◆ to deal with the unexpected.

The team will need to meet together regularly. I can't emphasize this enough. One of the quickest ways to destroy the working relationship of a team is only to meet when either the team leader believes it is necessary, or when one of the team members has a problem. (See Chapter 27 for further information about team building.) The dynamics quickly change from a regular, careful monitoring of the plan to either the feeling that 'we only meet when there's a problem', or 'we're only here to endorse the leader's good ideas'.

The only thing that now remains is to execute your plan. Given all the careful preparation that has gone into it, it should now run like a well-oiled train down railway lines. But there still remain a number of things that can derail it, even at this stage. These include:

◆ other people's last-minute 'good ideas'

◆ failure to watch the budget

◆ failure to initiate things in time

- pressure from others to change
- your own nervousness.

Whether you are on your own, or whether you are working with a team, the key task during this final stage of your communications plan is to keep the boundaries intact. This means making sure that:

- things are initiated on time
- the budget is not exceeded
- there are sufficient people to do the job
- the plan is monitored and measured as it progresses.

As people get involved with the task, they will inevitably come up with good ideas, and the more forceful of them will press hard for the plan to incorporate them. Each suggestion needs to be listened to, especially if it comes from younger members of the church (who often have a clarity of vision beyond the older ones, and who are often more in touch with their own culture), and considered on its merits. But it must meet the criteria that have already been defined and it can only be incorporated if it can be achieved without (a) exceeding the budget, and (b) deflecting the rest of the plan.

However, there will be times when, in the middle of executing a carefully thought-out plan, someone says, 'Why don't we do this?' If your team is meeting regularly, the response might well be: 'We will certainly consider it at the next team meeting.' If your team is meeting regularly, and the 'good idea' is still too urgent to wait until then, the chances are that it's too late!

WHEN TO MODIFY

There will inevitably be times when the plan needs to be modified. Here are some good reasons to change.

INSUFFICIENT RESOURCES

Perhaps the final quotations are well over budget. Or it becomes clear that there is not enough time to complete the execution. Perhaps the team have underestimated the amount of work that needs to be done, and there aren't enough people. If any of these happen, there should be an immediate re-working of the plan to correct it. It is no good continuing with a communications plan, no matter how good, if there are insufficient resources of time, money or energy to make it work. Disaster, both practical and personal, are waiting at the end of that path.

If there is a problem with resources, and it looks as though the plan might have to be modified as a result, this should be reported to the church council, or whatever body has oversight of the 'publicity team'. They not only deserve to know, but they might be able to offer some help towards a solution. If you have been reporting back on a regular basis, then these difficulties should not come as a shock. Besides, treated the right way, such an oversight team will usually be supportive, and will work with you to find a solution.

INADEQUATE RESPONSE

If you are monitoring the results of your plan against carefully pre-determined success factors, there should be a point during the execution when you either sit back and congratulate yourself and the team on the way the plan is achieving its aims, or you get increasingly concerned that it is not. Examine your feelings. Is this nagging worry based on hard evidence, or is it a result of nervousness because you are working in (what is for you) new, uncharted territory?

Ask yourself the following questions:

◆ What, exactly, is worrying me?

◆ Is there any evidence to support the worry?

◆ Where, according to the plan, should we be by now?

◆ Is the plan wrong, or over-optimistic?

◆ Do we need to consider any changes?

The same set of questions can be used with the team, if necessary. If the conclusion is that, despite a reasonable execution of the plan, it is not having the results that were expected, perhaps the time has come to modify, or to make those changes that are actually possible.

A note of caution here. It is possible, on those occasions when it seems sensible to modify the plan, to allow nerves (or sheer panic!) to blind both team and team leader to the resource implications of proposed changes. The first question to ask when any change is suggested is:

◆ Do we have enough time, money and energy to achieve this particular change?

Again, if you are reporting back on a regular basis to a church council or an oversight group, this can be a real help. You will need to maintain their confidence in your team and your plan, and nothing is more damaging to confidence than management by surprise! No one should expect a communications plan to work perfectly the first time, so a careful analysis of any difficulties, together with proposed solutions, should be given to those in authority, and the changes should be owned by those in authority. That way, no one should complain when things are done differently.

ADVERSE COMMENT

Be careful here. You have received considerable adverse comment on the plan as it begins to be executed. Where is the criticism coming from? Is it:

◆ from members of the target group?

◆ from members of your church?

If the adverse criticism is coming from those for whom the plan is designed—from the target audience—then it needs to be taken seriously, and the plan probably needs to be reviewed.

If, however, the adverse criticism is coming from people other than your target group, you need to be aware of a possible culture gap between the two groups. Where this happens, you need to do four things:

◆ discover the reaction of your target group, and see whether it reflects the same criticism

◆ check with those who are making the criticism to see exactly why they are critical

◆ check with those who are not making the criticism, to see how widespread are the complaints

◆ decide whether to make changes, or whether to explain your reasoning through an internal communication exercise.

The following example will help to illustrate these points:

A church decided to run an advertising campaign aimed at 16–21 year olds outside regular church membership to raise awareness of the church youth work. An advertising agency gave its time at a reduced fee, and came up with a sharp, witty slogan for posters and local radio. All those working on the campaign were delighted. But when the posters were printed, and the local radio started broadcasting the adverts, the church leaders began to get complaints from the church members that the campaign was 'unsuitable'.

The complaints were centred on the posters. When the communication team began to investigate, the first question they asked was why there were no complaints about the radio ads, which were potentially even more 'unsuitable'! Those complainants who were questioned said that they didn't listen to the radio station, and so hadn't heard the ads. Equally, those aged 16–21 from the church who were questioned were delighted with the campaign. They said that at last they felt that the church was doing something that they could defend!

The conclusion was that there was a considerable 'culture gap' between the complainants and the target group, and an internal communication exercise was mounted to present the campaign to the whole church, and to explain its aims. It was left to the internal process of church members discussing the campaign amongst themselves to counter the criticism, on the grounds that there would always be some who would disagree, but that the best defence would come from those church members who agreed with the campaign.

NEVER REACT DIRECTLY TO CRITICISM

It is easy to hear complaints, especially when they are made in a strident way, and to assume that those complaints are widely held. We often forget that those who are content, or even pleased, with a campaign rarely say so. But those who are opposed usually do. The first step is always to find out what proportion of the particular group is holding a critical or destructive view.

Having put the critical comments in perspective, seek to understand what lies behind the criticism. It may be there is a lack of understanding, or even communication, between the team and those who are making the critical comments. Even if the critics are in the majority, it doesn't necessarily mean that the plan should be changed. Maybe they don't understand what is being attempted, or simply haven't had a chance to question and 'own' the plan.

Often a carefully designed, swiftly executed internal presentation about the plan can change criticism to support, and enhance individual learning in the process.

KEEPING THE TEAM GOING

When there is criticism of any aspect of the communications plan, especially during its execution, this can have a debilitating effect on team members. This is where the regular meetings of the team will have paid off. The criticisms can be raised and faced at the regular team meetings without members feeling that they have been called together especially because of a 'crisis'. Individual concerns can be met, and a plan of action agreed.

Do not allow your team to disintegrate because individual members feel vulnerable to the criticism. Allow those fears to be expressed, and allow other members of the team to be supportive.

The execution phase of the communication plan will be a time when both team members and the team leader will feel under pressure. Working under pressure is never easy, and the pressure needs to be recognized. Now, more than ever, there needs to be space for regular prayer, for supporting individual team members, and for making priority decisions about the use of time. It is at this point that the team leader will discover whether he or she has allowed sufficient time in the plan to maintain the internal communication process.

Executing the communications plan is probably the most nerve-racking of all the steps. So far it has been a matter of theory and discussion. Now comes the acid test! Remember, God takes those things that we offer in good faith, and weaves them all into the rich tapestry of his kingdom.

MEASURING THE RESULTS 12

HOW HAVE WE DONE?

The execution is completed, and the team sits back to survey the results. How have they done? If success factors have been determined in advance, and set out as part of a written communication plan, they can be used to measure the success of the plan. But first, there needs to be a meeting of the team to review what has been achieved. During this meeting, time will need to be given for:

◆ individual members to share their feelings

◆ particular disasters (if any) to be given a ritual funeral and buried

◆ success to be celebrated

◆ further measurement to be planned, together with final conclusions and their dissemination.

THE LEARNING CURVE

The process of design, execution and reflection is a well-known process, and can be described in terms of the learning curve.

It is important, both for the well-being of the team members and their leader, and for the health of the church or group funding the communications plan, that there should be a serious attempt at measuring the results, and at feeding those results and the attendant conclusions back to the team and to the church.

Measurement can take place in a number of ways, and need be neither expensive nor complex. Some straightforward ways of measuring include:

◆ a simple questionnaire

◆ a 'focus' group

◆ a 'before and after' count

◆ an awareness test

◆ a few structured conversations.

A SIMPLE QUESTIONNAIRE

In drawing up a questionnaire, the following things need to be decided:

- What is to be measured?
- What will the results be used for?
- Who is to be asked?
- How will the results be analysed?
- Who will do the work?

There should be a real correlation between the various success criteria that have been decided in advance, and the thing to be measured. For example:

Plan A

Seven churches in one particular town had got together to run a campaign to bring new members into their youth groups.

Aim: *to bring new young people into youth groups in the seven churches of one town*

Success: *increase attendance by fifteen per cent or more*

Measure *(a) a simple 'before and after' count*
(b) feelings of youth leaders
(c) feelings of young people

Or:

Plan B

Aim: *to raise awareness of the church activities in the local community*

Success: *increased awareness amongst target groups measured by knowledge of the activities*

Measure: *an 'awareness' test conducted both before and after the exercise*

Both the above examples show the need for two sets of measurement. A base line needs to be established before the communication plan is executed, and then the increase in attendance or awareness needs to be measured against that base line.

The following simple questionnaire was designed for youth leaders to complete so as to measure the success or failure of the communications plan A:

1 Weekly attendance before the campaign

Please write down the attendance figures for each of the following evenings (before the campaign):

Week 1 _____   Week 2 _____   Week 3 _____   Week 4 _____

2 Weekly attendance during the campaign

Please write down the attendance figures for each of the following evenings (during the campaign):

Week 5 _____   Week 6 _____   Week 7 _____   Week 8 _____

3 Weekly attendance after the campaign

Please write down the attendance figures for each of the following evenings (after completion of the campaign):

Week 9 _____   Week 10 _____   Week 11 _____   Week 12 _____

4 On a scale of 1–5 (very negative, negative, neutral, positive, very positive) how did you feel about the campaign:

(a) Before it took place: _____   (b) During the campaign _____   (c) After the campaign _____

5 Roughly now many of the following groups of people mentioned the campaign to you:

(a) Existing members _____

(b) New members _____

6 Are you aware of any young people coming to your youth club as a direct result of the campaign:
YES ☐ NO ☐

If YES, how many? _____

A second simple questionnaire was produced for the members of the youth groups to complete:

1 Which youth group do you attend?

_____

2 Were you a member of the youth group before the campaign?
YES ☐ NO ☐

3 Were you aware of the campaign?
YES ☐ NO ☐

4 How did you feel about the campaign (please tick one box)?

Very positive ☐   Positive ☐   No feelings ☐

Negative ☐   Very negative ☐

By a simple analysis of the results, it is fairly straightforward to measure the success or failure of this particular campaign. Try designing a simple questionnaire to test the success of a campaign to achieve plan B above.

'FOCUS' GROUPS

A focus group can be used when you want to find out about people's feelings, their concerns, the issues they believe are important, rather than obtaining hard data. Running a focus group well is a professional skill, and should be approached with a degree of caution. But with a bit of planning, most people can put together a reasonable group and run it in a way that gains at least some results. A focus group is often used to help form questions that are tested by a questionnaire.

You will need to decide the following:

◆ Which group or groups are to be tested?

◆ What do you want to find out?

◆ How many groups should you run?

Example

A church ran a campaign to raise awareness and change attitudes of people towards homelessness.

Aim: to make people more aware of housing issues and to provoke action to increase the amount of single-person accommodation
Success: increased awareness in the community and the beginning of action to provide housing
Measure: (a) a focus group before campaign
(b) A focus group after campaign

Three groups of people were selected from the community: housewives, students and businessmen. Six people from each group were invited to attend a focus group by the following letter:

St Mark's Church, Anytown, would like to find out more about what people who live in Anytown think about their community, and what improvements we can make. We are running a number of 'focus groups' and would like to invite you to take part in one of these groups.

The groups will meet from 8.00 p.m. to 10.00 p.m. on Mondays during October at 34, Marsh Close, Anytown, the home of Mr and Mrs Smith. The evening will take the form of a structured discussion about our town, and the conversation will be tape-recorded for further analysis, though nothing will be made public that will identify any particular participant.
A member of our church will contact you shortly to ask whether you are willing to take part.

Before running a group with members of the public, it can help if a dummy run is held with members of the church. That way, any wrinkles in the process can be identified and any problems ironed out before 'going public'.

The leader needs to be someone other than the host, and needs to have a list of questions which will stimulate discussion, but also needs to be sufficiently skilled and confident to lead the conversation into areas which are exposed by the discussion. The task of the leader is:

◆ to hold the boundaries of the evening (time, courtesy, subject matter, confidentiality)

◆ to create a relaxed environment so that

people feel free to speak
- ◆ to engage all the members of the group
- ◆ to discover what members of the group feel and think about the issues being researched.

At the end of the evening, the participants need to be thanked, and the researcher needs to take the tape recording so as to draw up a report on the attitudes of the group, together with some possible questions for testing by a questionnaire (for example, what percentage of the community believes that there is no problem with homelessness?).

Running focus groups can be stimulating and fun, but they are not for those of a nervous disposition.

A 'BEFORE AND AFTER' COUNT

This is the simplest of all forms of measurement, and can either be incorporated in a questionnaire or used by itself. One simple example of a 'before and after' count is the person standing at the door of the church counting the number of people coming in. 'Before' he starts the church is empty, and 'after' he has finished, it holds a certain number of adults and a certain number of children!

The same exercise can be done over several weeks of a campaign, and the results compared. However, the results should carry a health warning, because without other forms of testing it is not possible to say that increases (or decreases) are a result of the campaign. There might be a correlation between the two, but it takes other forms of research to demonstrate cause and effect. Just because the numbers attending a church increase during a campaign, it does not mean that the publicity has been the cause. It might be simply that church members have invited their friends!

AN AWARENESS TEST

This is simply a matter of showing a pre-determined sample of people a series of pictures. Included in those pictures is one of the poster, or advertisement, or magazine cover (it could be anything that is able to be represented on paper). The numbers of people who recognize whatever it is that is being tested are recorded, and the test is repeated throughout the campaign so as to make a graph of (hopefully) increasing awareness.

A FEW STRUCTURED CONVERSATIONS

There are times when any form of structured research could be detrimental to the main aim of the campaign. If, for example, a campaign is being run to introduce people to church worship, it would hardly be appropriate (and probably counter-productive) to give all those attending a questionnaire. There may also be insufficient time or resources for more structured research.

At such times, a simple and effective way of measuring is for one or two people to engage others in conversation, gently asking one simple question during the course of the conversation designed to find out the desired information. It's the kind of research that the team leader can do himself or herself, and should not relied on as anything other than a simple indicator. But, like the focus group, it can be very revealing!

DISSEMINATING THE RESULTS

Your research will give a range of answers to the question 'How have we done?', and they need to be fed back, first to the communication team, then to the church, and where appropriate to the wider community. This reporting back is an important part of the process, because only when people know about the results can they own the success or learn from the failure. Be honest about the results. If they are inconclusive, or disappointing, then say so. And above all, use them as data for feeding back into the learning curve.

GOSPEL CRITERIA FOR MEASURING

Jesus himself told parables about measuring results. One such was the parable of the sower. It can be a healthy exercise to bear in mind that even the most successful campaign is likely to produce results similar to the sower.

'Listen! A farmer went out to sow his seed. As he was scattering the seed, some fell along the path, and the birds came and ate it up. Some fell on rocky places, where it did not have much soil. It sprang up quickly, because the soil was shallow. But when the sun came up, the plants were scorched, and they withered because they had no root. Other seed fell among thorns, which grew up and choked the plants, so that they did not bear grain. Still other seed fell on good soil. It came up, grew and produced a crop, multiplying thirty, sixty, or even a hundred times.'

Then Jesus said, 'He who has ears to hear, let him hear.'

Mark 4:3–9 (NIV)

SECTION TWO
MEDIA OPTIONS

13 THE MEDIA AT YOUR DISPOSAL

WHAT ARE 'THE MEDIA'?

Talk about 'the media', and most people automatically think of television, radio and newspapers—usually in that order. But the word 'media' comes from the root word behind 'medium' and 'mediation'. The media are those channels of communication which mediate between one person and another, or between one group and another. With the advent of satellite communication, the mediation can now be between one nation and another, or even one continent and another.

Mediation is not a static word. It conveys the sense of active, rather than passive communication. There is a process of negotiation taking place. The mediator takes the trouble to interpret between two people or two groups of people, conveying the meaning of the one to help the other understand. There is a translation taking place which is actively seeking the involvement of each party, actively working to convey meaning between two unlike groups.

The specific choice of one medium over another needs to be made with at least some understanding of how this translation process differs from medium to medium. The use of television, for example, to mediate between two groups of people involves a different 'translation process' than, say, the use of the telephone. The medium may operate by bringing two individuals very close together, or it may operate by keeping them apart. It may, like a poster, translate by the use of pictures and feelings; or it may, like a newspaper or a book, translate entirely by words and concepts. In the medium of television, the producer works by using pictures and words to convey both meaning and feeling; he or she translates between that which is filmed and the viewer. It is the personal selection of material, of style, of presentation, that is at work; the producer makes choices between different sets of pictures, between different sets of words, and both the hidden assumptions and explicit intentions of the producer influence what is received.

This process of translation is rarely 'clean', in the sense that there is a third party involved who may well be 'contaminated' by a particular culture, a set of values or personal issues. The editor or producer who negotiates the translation of an issue or a story between subject and audience may have a particular message of his or her own, which acts on both language and content. Equally, the medium itself may operate in a way that colours the translation process.

No media can therefore be value-free. In the messages that are conveyed, in the culture and bias of the editor or producer of those messages, and in the nature of the medium itself, there are sets of values which may, or may not, be consonant with the values of the Christian community.

This understanding of 'media' as a means of translation is paralleled in the Christian understanding of incarnation. For the Christian communicator, the model with which we work is one of incarnation and vulnerability. Nowhere is this model better portrayed than in Paul's letter to the Philippians (2:5–11):

Your attitude should be the same as that of Christ Jesus: Who, being in very nature God, did not consider equality with God something to be grasped, but made himself nothing, taking the very nature of a servant, being made in human likeness. And being found in appearance as a man, he humbled himself and became obedient to death—even death on a cross!

Therefore God exalted him to the highest place and gave him the name that is above every name, that at the name of Jesus every knee should bow, in heaven and on earth and under the earth, and every tongue confess that Jesus Christ is Lord, to the glory of God the Father.

This also is the model of the community of faith within which God himself continues his mediating work in the world. It is within this community of faith that the values and choices we make are tested against the one who mediates between God and humanity. This is the model which authenticates our media choices both as consumers and users, and it is against these values that we test each media choice we make.

WHAT IS MEDIATED?

With a few limited exceptions, what is mediated between originator and audience is 'story'. The news programmes on radio and television and the news section of the newspapers are made up of a series of short 'stories', carefully crafted to inform or disturb across a range of human experience, and are presented as complete in themselves.

News stories are, of course, only 'snapshots' in a continuing process of human experience. Each of these stories is incomplete in the sense that they fail to show the complexity of what happened before, what actions or neglect led up to these 'crisis points' in human concerns, and often leave the viewer, listener or reader without an understanding of their resolution. And like someone showing his holiday slides to a neighbour, it is up to the news editor to choose which of them we will see, hear or read about. The experience of the news story is often incomplete, partial and unresolved.

This is why another form of 'story', the documentary, is both important and popular. In an hour or so, the issues can be looked at in considerable depth. The issues of actions that led up to the 'crisis point' can be explored, and its resolution discussed. The television or radio documentary finds its newspaper parallel in the extended feature or report.

Drama and soap on television and radio, and the serial in a newspaper or magazine, are other forms of story. These are fictional, but still convey values and model a way of behaving which some media commentators suggest provide powerful alternative 'parent models' for the resolution of human conflict. *Grange Hill*, a serial programme broadcast on British television made for young teenagers, and based on the conflicts and opportunities of life in a state secondary school, received a mixture of criticism and acclaim for the behaviour it modelled and the authenticity it supposedly conveyed.

USING THE MEDIA APPROPRIATELY

From these basic concepts we can move on to outline a number of principles that the Christian communicator can use to test his or her use of the media. As far as possible, it should be:

◆ honest

◆ non-manipulative

◆ open to response

◆ based on story

◆ engaged with human experience.

It is at this point that the Christian communicator faces his or her first major dilemma. Much of the Christian story is hidden. On a number of occasions Jesus told people 'not to tell' who he was or what he had done. He certainly resisted the use of miracles (or, to use John's word, 'signs') as propaganda for his ministry. In fact, this was one of the temptations that had to be resisted. 'If you are the Son of God, cast yourself off the temple...' Matthew records Jesus' instruction to his disciples: 'Do not give dogs what is sacred; do not throw your pearls to pigs. If you do, they may trample them under their feet, and then turn and tear you to pieces.'

The stories of the Gospels are about discovery, not propaganda. Through their experience of this person Jesus, his followers came to discover truth about themselves, about him and about God. Much of that discovery was personal, and was reflected in a change of direction. What changed the direction was often hidden, and demanded enquiry from others. Suggestions that Jesus should demonstrate who he was by working miracles, or that he should avoid the pain of crucifixion, were rejected, and his disciples were warned to avoid this temptation.

We have to take that warning seriously. A headlong rush to use the media to demonstrate or 'prove' that God is still at work in his world will receive the same condemnation today.

How then can the Christian community use the media appropriately? There are four basic ways that conform to Jesus' own ministry:

◆ challenge wrongdoing

◆ affirm right behaviour and thinking

◆ tell stories which point towards God

◆ live the gospel in a way that invites comment.

The following chapters in this section describe in detail how to use the various sorts of media available to us. Each operates in a different way, and that difference is usually found in the way the medium 'translates' between the event and the viewer, listener or reader. Understand the translation process, and you have largely understood the medium.

GAINING ACCESS TO THE PRINTED AND BROADCAST MEDIA 14

The printed and broadcast media of press, radio and television are the most powerful forms of mass communication. Between them, these three media reach millions of people across the world, bringing information, education and entertainment in what has become a vast business enterprise.

Press, radio and television have a huge influence on today's society. Their programmes and articles raise awareness of issues, challenge set opinions and, like a terrier after a rat, worry away at those who they believe have something to hide. They are a vital guardian of our freedom, and reflect every section of society. By their very nature, newspapers, radio and television stations exploit controversy, and thrive on division and conflict. They devour information and repackage it in a hundred different ways.

Because the church is part of the society in which they operate, we are of interest not only when things go wrong, but when we speak on matters of faith, of morals, or of politics. We are part of the community that challenges authority, or does newsworthy things. But it is up to us to make sure that we have a fair share of the output!

The good communicator always uses press, radio and television as media through which to speak to specific groups of people, and never as an end in itself. Although it's nice (sometimes) to see your church's photograph in the paper, or to hear your story on radio, the purpose of proactive use is always to communicate to the other readers and listeners through the medium of the newspaper, radio or television: never simply 'to get my story in'. Different media attract different groups of people, and newspapers in particular are aimed at different levels of readership and different political stances. Some are read by the financially influential; some by white- or blue-collar workers; some by teachers and intellectuals.

Gathering an audience of influential people is not something that is entirely limited to newspapers. There is one radio programme which also has an influence out of all proportion to its audience size, precisely for this reason. In the United Kingdom, BBC Radio 4's *Today* programme broadcast from 6.30 a.m. to 9.00 a.m. on weekday mornings is listened to by politicians, industrialists, leading civil servants, and other major decision-makers, and has a huge 'agenda setting' function.

Television can act to influence in a different way. The special nature of television, its unique translation process, is found in the combination of sound and pictures edited in a way that concentrates much more on emotions. The stories conveyed by television demand our total attention, and act directly on our feelings as well as our thinking. So a television documentary can have a huge influence on a community not only through the logical statement of disturbing facts, but in the raising of anger or distress in millions of people.

For most churches, the commonest points of access to the printed and broadcast media are:

◆ through the news desk

◆ through a news agency

◆ through the picture desk

◆ through a known contact or specialist reporter.

THE NEWS DESK

Most newspapers and television and radio stations have a news desk staffed by professional journalists responsible for gathering potential stories for inclusion in the output. These days, few news journalists have to go looking for stories—they come pouring in from a number of sources:

◆ news agencies

◆ public relations (PR) specialists

◆ news releases

◆ other media

◆ private individuals

◆ commerce and industry.

That many news journalists still do go out into the community looking for news is a continuing sign of the health of the media. Yet many news desks, especially in commercial radio where the pressure on finances means that staffing is cut to the bone, operate by telephone, reacting to stories that are sent to them from the news agencies to which they subscribe.

Getting a church or religious story into the news is a matter of combining four things:

◆ knowing what makes a good news story

◆ knowing who to contact

◆ knowing how to contact them and when

◆ knowing how to put the story across.

KNOWING WHAT MAKES NEWS

News journalists describe news in all sorts of ways, but the first task for the church communicator is knowing what is, and what is not, news. Here are a few definitions of news that I have heard, all from senior practising news journalists:

◆ news is extraordinary things happening to ordinary people, or ordinary things happening to extraordinary people

◆ news is what some people don't want other people to know

◆ news is what gets talked about in the pub

◆ news is about what changes people's lives

◆ news is about controversy and challenge to authority.

So, to use the classic definition, a story about a dog biting a man is not news, unless the man is famous. But what about a man biting a dog?

KNOWING WHO TO CONTACT

Almost without exception, your first contact will be with a news journalist. These are people whose job it is to make quick decisions about what might, or might not, be a good news story. You should start by:

◆ making a list of all the media in your area

◆ looking up their telephone numbers

◆ finding out the fax number of their news room.

Often the first thing to overcome is fear. Remember that journalists want to hear from you. You will not be 'bothering' them, or putting them out. You may well have the news story that is sufficiently 'out of the ordinary' to make the front page, or the lead story in their evening news bulletin. Besides, newspapers, radio and television have an insatiable appetite for news. Like some teenagers, there's never a time when they have had enough. Day after day, week after week, they have to fill vast numbers of pages or huge stretches of time with stories that are different, entertaining, tragic, disturbing. Your story might well be included simply because it's there on the news editor's desk when he or she needs something different!

After a while, you can build up a working relationship with local journalists and this can be mutually beneficial. If you have taken on the job of press contact for your church, the first thing you need to do is to get to know your local journalists. You could invite them for a pub lunch, or at least call into the office of your local newspaper or radio station and introduce yourself to the news editor.

KNOWING HOW TO CONTACT THEM AND WHEN

There are a number of traditional ways of contacting a journalist with a news story. You can:

◆ send a news release

◆ make a telephone call

◆ call a news conference

The news release

Out of all the methods of informing the media of a story, the most basic tool is the news release. This is simply an outline of the story which has all the basic facts, and from which the news journalist can decide on its news value and what further work needs to be done. A good news release has the following information, though not necessarily in this order:

◆ what is happening

◆ when it is happening

◆ where it is happening

◆ why it is happening

◆ who is involved.

News releases should be typed, on one side of the paper only, with double spacing and a wide margin. They should always carry the name and telephone number of the person to be contacted for further information about the story, usually at the bottom of the release.

The story should be summed up in the first paragraph, and then each subsequent paragraph should expand on the different aspects of the story, in decreasing order of importance. Some journalists like news releases to be written so that they can be incorporated almost unchanged into the newspaper or radio bulletin, others simply like the outline on which they can work. Experience will tell.

News releases can be faxed or posted to the chosen journalists or news desks; it is rarely cost-effective to send them by messenger even though a number of messenger services exist for this purpose. But they do need to be sent in good time: two, possibly three days before the event itself.

The telephone call

This is often the best way of making a first contact with the news desk. You have the journalist's immediate attention, and about two minutes to explain what your story is and why you think he or she might be interested in it. You should:

◆ write down the important points of your story

◆ if you have time, write a news release

◆ telephone the media outlet and ask for the news desk

◆ explain your story to the journalist succinctly, using the five 'w's outlined on page 73

◆ if the journalist asks you to send him or her a copy of your news release, ask to whom it should be sent, and send it right away, by fax if possible

◆ if he or she doesn't ask for a copy, ask whether it would be welcomed by someone else—the religious producer, for example.

The telephone call is an excellent way of working with the media. Many journalists are bombarded by news releases and public relations guff by the yard. Local authorities use up acres of fax paper with endless reports of council meetings. Even a good news release has to compete for a journalist's time. Send a news release unannounced, and it may well get missed. But a quick telephone call can help both sides. It gives the journalist the opportunity to make an instant decision, and alerts him or her to a possible news story. And it means that he or she is watching out for your news release. My practice is to telephone the journalist with the basis of the story, ask if he or she would like a news release (the answer is invariably 'yes'), and then make a follow-up call a day later.

Calling a news conference

A news conference is a gathering of journalists from various media outlets so that they can all be briefed or updated on a story at the same time. It is used to launch a major initiative, to announce a new senior appointment (but only when the person appointed can be present), or to give information in the aftermath of a serious difficulty or disaster. It is a convenience for the journalists, who have the opportunity to put questions directly, and get the story at the same time as their competitors, and it is a convenience to the organizers, who can generate a large amount of media interest, but contain most of it within a short time-scale.

Call a news conference when there is likely to be considerable media interest in the story. The following things need to be done before the conference:

◆ The time of the conference needs to be fixed to suit media deadlines. This is often early in the week to suit the weeklies, and during the morning to suit the dailies.

- Arrange for a suitable venue with seating for sufficient numbers.
- Identify and brief the main speakers (two speakers and a chairperson is an ideal number).
- Draw up a media list and send out invitations to journalists in good time.
- Prepare a news release for those attending, and for those who are unable to attend but who want the story anyway.
- A few days before the conference, telephone the journalists to find out if they are attending. This can stimulate memories, and discover where the original invitation has failed to find its intended recipient.
- Warn the participants that they will be photographed.

These days there is little point in spending money on lavish entertainment. Journalists are busy working people, and those journalists who are going to make the most use of the conference are the ones that leave quickly to get the story out. A cup of tea or coffee on arrival is welcome, but more than this is usually unnecessary.

The layout of the room is important:

- Provide a solid table for the speakers to sit behind. Not only does this act as a focus for the conference, but it provides psychological security for the speakers, and a place for radio and other journalists to place microphones and recorders.
- Provide name plaques which are clearly visible for each person sitting at the table.
- Leave a good amount of space between the first row of chairs and the table to allow photographers and sound engineers to operate.
- Leave a central aisle between the seats for people to move in and out during the conference.
- Provide space for television cameras and crews, either at the rear behind the seats, or in reserved spaces at the sides.

On the day of the conference, the following tasks need to be done, and are the responsibility of the person chairing the conference:

- check sound re-enforcement equipment (if any)
- keep an attendance list
- maintain time boundaries
- Ensure that no single journalist is allowed to dominate the questions.

The usual format for a news conference is as follows:

- the main speakers are introduced by name and position
- the leading speaker makes the announcement, and is backed up by the second (where necessary)
- opportunities are given by the chair for questions
- the chairperson brings the questions to a close, and arranges a photo call
- following the photo call, individual interviews are organized by the chairperson where requested.

For some occasions, it is more suitable to have the photo call before the main conference: where, for example, the action takes place outside, and the conference inside.

After the conference is over, the attendance list needs to be compared with the original invitation list, and those who were unable to attend need to be sent the news release by fax.

Producing a briefing pack

For a major story that is likely to run for some time, or has a large number of relevant facts and figures, it can be very helpful for journalists if you produce a briefing pack. This can contain a basic news release, together with a paper with all the relevant facts and figures, and papers answering the most likely questions.

A question-and-answer sheet

Question-and-answer sheets are very useful not only for the journalist, but for briefing other members of the organization about a particular topic or issue. The various questions that a journalist or member of the public might ask are typed out, and immediately below is given the answer that any representative of the organization might give, together with any relevant facts and figures.

Quotes

Quotes are either 'attributed' to someone, or are non-attributable. The source of an attributable quote is always a named person: Mr John Smith, Chairman of the Church Council, said: 'I am in favour of the plan.' A non-attributable quote is given either by someone who is expressing the view of an organization or another individual, and not his or her own view, or by someone who for other reasons is not prepared to be named: A spokesperson for the Diocese said: 'The Bishop is unable to approve the plan because . . .'

On and off the record

Sometimes, all a journalist needs to do is to be able to understand a particular issue or situation. If it seems from the questions that the journalist doesn't understand the problem, or is being unnecessarily hostile, it can sometimes help to suggest an 'off the record' briefing.

Whatever is said 'off the record' is for the journalist only, and not for publication, so you need to be very careful about using this technical device. Always ask: 'Would it help if I spoke off the record?' You must have the journalist's agreement first, but once he or she has agreed, then you can relax a bit, and brief the journalist as fully as you are able.

Always check from time to time that you are still 'off the record', and when the briefing is finished, be sure to confirm when you are going back 'on the record'. In my experience, an 'off the record' briefing is warmly appreciated by most journalists, and helps them to frame sensible questions which you can then answer 'on the record'.

The embargo

The embargo is used in those cases where a journalist is going to need time to prepare background information in advance of a major statement. It is not for the convenience of the press officer or church communicator. A typical use of an embargo is when the honours list is published. Journalists need time to interview the recipients of honours, and to obtain their photographs, so the list is published 'under embargo' until a certain date and time.

Embargoed stories should not appear in print, or on radio or television, until the embargo has expired. It is also a matter of integrity that the journalist does not discuss an embargoed matter with those who are not professionally concerned with the story. This is what an embargo looks like:

EMBARGOED
until 00.01 a.m., Monday 7 November

Always be specific with an embargo, and make sure that it appears on every page of the news release or other material that is sent to journalists. Embargoes should only be used for a few days, and if someone either inadvertently or deliberately breaks an embargo, the other news media may also run the story.

THE NEWS AGENCY

News is a saleable commodity, and there are a number of specialist news agencies whose main function is to gather news stories and sell them to press, radio and television outlets. The news agencies provide a service for the national, regional and local media by providing them with accurate, immediate news stories that the individual newspapers, radio and television stations can use. In the old days, the agencies used a form of telex to transmit their stories, which came 'off' or 'down' the wire. Today, most agencies use a computer link for their stories.

Getting a story run by one of the news agencies is one way of making sure that every media outlet in the UK has access to it. In the UK, the Press Association (or PA as it is usually called) is the major domestic agency, and Reuters is the major international agency. Stories should be sent to a national news agency only if they are likely to be of national interest. There are a number of smaller, regional news agencies specializing in local news, and these can sometimes be helpful.

But, like many things in this world, it's a case of 'buyer beware'. The media does have its less attractive side, and some of these small, local agencies make their money by selling unsavoury stories to the seamier tabloid press. Where these agencies are known to sell such stories, it can sometimes be a helpful policy not to use them, and to on some occasions to refuse to work with them.

Often, the biggest barrier to contacting a news room or a journalist is simply the fear of picking up the phone. All of us, at some time or other, have hesitated because we weren't quite sure what to do, or how we would be received. Remember, most newspapers and television and radio stations are hungry for material. They will be glad of your call, and even if they don't use the particular story you are offering today, they may well come back to you at another time because they will (if they are switched on) have put your name in their contacts book.

15 TELEVISION AS A MEDIUM

The medium of television can be sub-divided into its types:

◆ terrestrial (direct from transmitter to aerial)

◆ satellite (indirect via satellite)

◆ cable (direct from source via cable)

and further, by its means of funding:

◆ public service, funded by licence fee (or in some countries, from taxes)

◆ independent, funded either by income from advertising sales, or by subscription, or by a combination of both.

Television can operate as an international medium, transmitting its programmes via a satellite in geostationary orbit which has a 'footprint' across several countries or even continents. One example of this is Cable News Network (CNN) which can be received across the world from its satellite distribution system. Normally funded by income from both advertising and programme sales, programmes distributed by satellite are planned for mass appeal, often worldwide appeal.

Television can operate as a national medium, either as a single public service channel or as a network of smaller, commercial companies with regionally made programmes scheduled into a national network. The Independent Television Network (ITN) in the UK is one such, made up of a number of smaller, independent regional companies making their own programmes.

Television can operate as a regional medium, with companies making news programmes reflecting the culture and editorial area of a particular region, and scheduled into a national network to provide local or regional news with which the viewer has more chance of identifying. Regional television in the UK is made by both BBC and independent television companies.

Television can also operate as a local medium. Cable companies operate in a growing number of towns and cities, transmitting their images quite literally along underground cables which enter individual houses. Cable companies transmit a variable number of channels, many of which, like their satellite counterparts, are dedicated to one particular type of programme. Amongst them in the UK can be found the Vision Channel, the UK's first Christian channel run by Fran Wildish, a visionary housewife from Swindon.

But it is here that things begin to get

complicated, because cable companies are offering their subscribers far more than local television. In practice, though the service may originate locally, and be limited to a few square miles, there may be very little truly local television at all. Cable operators are selling a package which includes both national and satellite television, telephone lines, and a host of other electronic features (such as local viewdata). The point of origin for cable television, the 'cable head' as it is known, may 'take down' a number of channels from different satellites according to demand and market forces, and although there may be a small investment in 'community programming', this form of local television usually relies (at least in the UK) on volunteers and has a very small audience. So cable television, rather than being a truly local television service, is more properly a television redistribution and marketing service.

At the moment in the UK, there are more homes with direct satellite receivers than with cable, although in the next few years cable is likely to overtake satellite as more and more towns are cabled. Both cable and, increasingly, satellite, are subscription services, with programmes encrypted to ensure that the programmes are paid for by viewers who have to buy an electronic 'card' to decrypt, or unscramble, the pictures.

Television is the most powerful medium, and the most difficult to access. It demands total attention, telling the story by pictures and sound. It acts on the emotions as well as the intellect, creating anger or dismay, delight or disturbance in millions of people at one time. It is more distant than newspapers or radio, and for most church communicators, television is about painting a broad picture for large numbers of people, rather than giving detailed information to more select audiences.

Because television conveys 'live' pictures of its subjects, there are messages being conveyed even before people speak. A minister appearing in a traditional cassock, seated in a book-lined study, gives one message: a minister in casual clothes, filmed in a busy high street, gives another. Both are speaking to the viewer before they open their mouths.

If you are invited to give a television interview, you need to prepare in much the same way as for a radio interview, but with one or two additions:

◆ Ask the person making the invitation exactly what the interview will be about, and why they are interested in you.

◆ Find out where and when the interview is to take place, how long it is likely to take, and who else is being interviewed.

◆ Ask yourself whether you are the right person to give the interview, or whether there is someone else who is the 'expert' and who might feel that he or she should have been asked.

◆ Prepare as thoroughly as you can. Don't take a prepared speech—it will look 'false', and will probably be unacceptable to the television company. A few headline 'notes' on one sheet of paper is acceptable as a prompt immediately before the interview, provided you don't refer to them during the interview itself.

◆ Decide in advance on two or three main points that you want to get across.

- Decide what 'image' you want to convey. Prepare to dress accordingly, and beware of being manipulated into a 'stereotype'.

TRAINING

If you feel you need training or experience, the national communication office of most churches can often provide training at fairly short notice. Television interviews can be daunting things if you are not used to them, and training can really help by giving you experience of how they work, and how to improve your performance.

Television interviews are always edited, and contributions which take up to half an hour to film can be condensed into as little as thirty seconds. The sheer unpredictability of the television interview is one reason why it can be so demanding on the person being interviewed.

NEWS CRITERIA

It is never easy to interest a regional television newsroom in a church story. Often, the church has been used as the 'tease' or oddball story at the bottom of the programme. On occasions, it has been the subject of controversy. The 'good' story needs the following in order even to be considered:

- Good pictures—television is fundamentally a picture service, and one of the first criteria for a news story is whether the producer can get good pictures to illustrate the story. It's no good having a superb story if it is impossible to illustrate with good footage.
- Regional or national interest—most television stations are at least regional, and the story needs to be of sufficient importance to interest the region.
- A 'strong' story—ask yourself: 'Is this story likely to get talked about in the pub or on the golf course?'

If your story has all of these characteristics, then it's worth telephoning the television news room and discussing it with the news editor.

OTHER TYPES OF TELEVISION PROGRAMME

There are other ways of using television to communicate apart from interviews. The growth of 'chat shows' and audience participation shows has generated two new access points. Again, it's worth telephoning the producer of any regional chat show and asking when they are planning to invite a representative of the Christian (or indeed, any religious) community.

Another way in is to telephone the production office of the audience discussion programme and ask how you can take part, and whether they are planning to discuss any of the topics in which you are particularly interested.

FILMING IN CHURCH

From time to time, both film and television companies need to film in church. This can be for a variety of reasons:

◆ news coverage

◆ drama production

◆ religious programmes

◆ advertising.

NEWS COVERAGE IN CHURCH

This is simply a matter of agreeing with the television company on the positioning of cameras, any lighting that might be required, and what may and may not be filmed. It helps to have a written agreement, but this can be simply in the form of a letter. Electronic news gathering has become so sophisticated that a tripod camera and a crew of two, without any extra lighting, is usually all that is required.

There are those who do not believe that television should be allowed in churches. In 1953, the then Archbishop of Canterbury was worried about the television broadcasting of the coronation of Queen Elizabeth II from Westminster Abbey because he thought that people might be watching with their hats on. Silly as this sounds today, there are still those who have difficulty in accepting television into churches and cathedrals.

It is a very exclusive attitude, and gives the impression that the worship of God is for an élite few, rather than for all. Many are unable to come to church, and for major events there simply will not be room for everyone who would like to attend. Appropriate pictures of a religious service on the news after a major disaster, or at a special time of celebration, can provide Christian focus for society, or an opportunity to give thanks to God.

FILMING IN CHURCH ON OTHER OCCASIONS

Drama, documentaries, advertising and film production all need to film in and around churches from time to time. If you are approached for permission to film:

◆ Ask to see the shooting script. This will tell you not only what words are being used, but what activities surround them. What might be entirely innocent words can be given an entirely new meaning by the activities of the actors!

◆ Make sure that the company has adequate insurance to cover any damage to the church, its contents and the churchyard. Check with your own insurers if you are uncertain what to ask.

◆ Ask what vehicles are going to be brought onto church property, and what is going to be moved or changed. One scene in the film *The Eagle has Landed* used a church in Berkshire where the director carefully removed the stained glass windows, put in false ones, then blew them out.

◆ Don't be afraid of negotiating appropriate fees. In the UK the Guild of

Location Managers can advise on the level of fees to charge.

CABLE TELEVISION

Many towns in the UK and elsewhere are now cabled, and the number of subscribers to cable television is set to overtake satellite in the next few years. However, few cable companies have their own local newsroom. Most are content to redistribute programmes provided by satellite companies. There are a few local community channels, but most are seriously underfunded, employ a volunteer team, and have a very small audience.

SATELLITE TELEVISION

In many ways this is entirely similar to national terrestrial television. The same rules apply, and contact is made through the news room. Because few churches currently make contact with the various satellite channels, they are very open to church news, but it does have to be at least of potential national interest.

THE AMATEUR VIDEO MAKER

Videos of weddings and other services can be a great help to the mission of the church.

◆ They allow absent friends and relatives to join in.

◆ They give the participants a lasting spiritual reminder of their service.

◆ They promote the ministry of the church.

However, amateur video makers can also be a nuisance to both ministers and worshippers if they are allowed to roam unchecked around a church during a service of worship. The following points should prevent the worst excesses:

◆ The church should have a clear policy on videography which is on public display.

◆ The policy should be explained, and preferably given in printed form, to those people wanting videos of church services.

◆ The videographer must obtain the appropriate copyright licences.

◆ Each videographer must be individually authorized for each service by the minister or someone appointed by him or her only on production of the appropriate copyright licences.

Video can be a useful tool for communication, and because so many people have access to home video cameras, and relatively easy access to editing facilities, it is possible for the average church to make quite acceptable videos on a range of subjects. In my own church, for example, we had difficulties in communicating about overseas mission. The problem was that people who had lived all their lives in an English cathedral city had absolutely no concept of Christianity in a culture completely alien to their own. Their lack of experience of that culture meant that they had no framework within which to make sense of the issues that the mission was raising.

This led to the formulation of yet another law of communication:

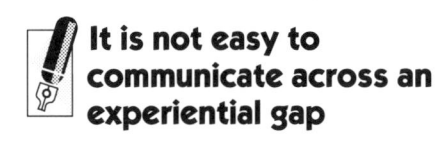

🖋 It is not easy to communicate across an experiential gap

It also led to a project to close that experiential gap. The idea was to use video to give people a real understanding of what it was like to work as a Christian missionary in an agricultural training centre in the Gambia, West Africa. We simply sent two members of the church to the Gambia, equipped with a home video camera, and asked them to film those things that would convey the most meaning to the other members of the church. They came back with a story to tell, and they themselves became the medium which translated between the two cultures. Their video footage, which was edited into an hour's programme, was shown in church and in the local primary school. It did wonders for the church's understanding of, and commitment to, overseas mission.

Television (as well as amateur and professional videography) is a powerful and emotive medium which communicates at an emotional level almost more than at an intellectual level. It may be that, because more energy is required to follow both pictures and words at the same time, less can be devoted to an intellectual analysis of the content. Or it might simply be that human beings are seduced into enjoyment of the story in a way that lulls our critical faculties into neutral. It can be the primary tool for translating between one culture to another, or it can be an emotive supporting medium for personal testimony. Used as a news medium, it can convey drama in a way that no other medium is able, but its limitation is that it paints in broad brush-strokes, rather than in detailed analysis.

16 RADIO AS A MEDIUM

Like television, the medium of radio can be subdivided into its types:

◆ terrestrial (direct from transmitter to aerial)

◆ satellite (indirect via satellite)

◆ cable (direct from source via cable)

and further, by its means of funding:

◆ public service, funded by licence fee (or in some countries, from taxes)

◆ independent, funded either by income from advertising sales, or by subscription, or by a combination of both

◆ community and restricted licence stations, where small-scale stations operate sometimes for as little as one weekend, and which cover a small area.

Radio operates as an international medium in much the same way as television. As well as the high-powered shortwave transmissions, there are a growing number of radio stations using the satellite network. Transmitted on a number of audio carriers alongside the television channels, there are many little-known radio stations. Amongst them can be found a few specifically Christian stations, such as United Christian Broadcasters (UCB), an offshoot of New Zealand's Radio Rhema, or World Radio Network, the Vatican's radio station.

Radio operates as a national medium, either as a public service channel (such as BBC Radios 1–4), or as a commercial channel (such as Classic FM). At present in the UK there is no national network of independent local or regional radio stations, although there is an independent news network, IRN (Independent Radio News), which is taken by most independent local radio stations.

Radio can also operate as a local medium, with independent stations funded from advertising income and public service provision funded from a licence fee. BBC Local Radio stations can be heard in most parts of the UK.

Increasingly, there is a move towards community radio, with stations operating on specially restricted licences for as little as one weekend, or (under current legislation in the UK) up to one month. These stations are funded in a whole variety of ways, from private donations or subscriptions to small-scale advertising income, or a mixture of all three. Community radio offers the local church a low-cost entry into radio broadcasting, because it is possible to run a special-event FM radio station during a mission or festival.

Radio is a very intimate medium. The

radio announcer may have an audience of thousands, or even millions, but he or she is speaking to one person. Radio is a flexible medium, allowing the imagination to paint pictures around a framework created by words and sounds. Radio is also a secondary activity: you can listen to the radio whilst you're driving the car or cooking the dinner,—something that is difficult with newspapers or television. Radio can convey emotion far better than newspapers, because you can hear the speakers' tone of voice, listen to the tension between speakers, or have your feelings changed through small silences or sound effects.

But it is also a very transitory medium. What you hear at one moment is gone forever a second later. Unless the programme is recorded there is no way of referring back to what has been said, and unless you leave a tape running throughout the day, you will sooner or later hear the tail end of an item that interests you greatly, and feel the frustration of not being able to refer back to it.

Radio is also a very accessible medium. There are large numbers of 'phone in' programmes, where listeners can make (almost) instant contributions to debates on a wide range of topics. A news story can be given to the radio station, and heard by large numbers of people within an hour. Interviews can be given over the telephone. A 'what's on' diary run by the local radio station gives an instant picture of events taking place in the locality that day.

BEING INTERVIEWED

Contact with the news room of a local radio station will usually result in a request for an interview, so it's no good sending a story to the radio station if there's no one willing to go 'on air'.

If you accept an invitation to give an interview, you need to do the following things:

◆ Ask the person making the invitation exactly what the interview will be about, and why they are interested in you.

◆ Find out where and when the interview is to take place, how long it is likely to take, and who else is being interviewed.

◆ Ask yourself whether you are the right person to give the interview, or whether there is someone else who is the 'expert' and who might feel that he or she should have been asked.

◆ Prepare as thoroughly as you can. Don't take a prepared speech, as that will sound 'false', and interviewers don't like them. A few headline 'notes' on one sheet of paper is acceptable.

◆ Decide in advance on two or three main points that you want to get across.

When you get to the studio, or when the reporter arrives at your home, double-check that the interview is still about what you thought it would be about. It is not unknown for the emphasis to change, or even for the reporter to get it wrong! Discuss the general shape of the interview with the reporter or producer. You have a right to know what the first question will be, so be prepared. Assuming all is well:

◆ Take some (discrete) deep breaths to calm yourself.

◆ Try to ignore the microphone, and treat the interviewer as your audience. Aim to convince him or her of the points you are making, rather than broadcasting to thousands.

◆ Be prepared for sharp questions. Often the reporter will take an opponent's position so as to draw out your argument. Don't be afraid of countering his or her arguments with your own: a little controversy will help your listeners grasp your position. The question, 'Many people want the freedom to shop on Sundays, don't they?' is an easier question to answer than the rather woolly, 'What do you think about Sunday shopping'?

◆ Don't feel restricted by the questions. Use them as an opportunity to make the points you have prepared in advance.

◆ Don't ramble. Keep your answers short and clear. This gives you an opportunity to say more, and helps avoid the editing out of points you wanted to make.

◆ Don't be afraid of repeating yourself if the reporter repeats similar questions. You could be being pushed to say more than you want to, or to contradict something you have already said.

THE 'THOUGHT FOR THE DAY'

If you are invited to give a 'thought for the day', again it is preparation that makes it work. The first thing to do is to listen to the other 'thoughts' that are being broadcast, and then to the rest of the station's output around that time. Is it made up of fast, up-beat, short news stories? If so, the station will want something that fits that format. Is it a more serious programme, with three-minute mini-features on different topics? If so, your 'thought' should fit that format by being slightly more serious, possibly slightly longer. If the output is mainly music, you might ask if a particular record could be played to lead out of your 'thought'.

Prepare well, and write out your script in the style that you will read it. We tend not to use 'do not' or 'can not' in conversation: we use 'don't', or 'can't'. Your script should look as though it is speech, not writing. If in any doubt, you can ask the producer of the programme to look at your script and make suggestions on its style. Use examples, stories, surprise, humour and anecdotes to help make your point. It is not a news story, and it rarely helps to criticize others. Remember, the vast majority of listeners will not be regular church-goers, and will respond much better to thoughts related to everyday experience, rather than the more restricted 'church speak'.

RUNNING YOUR OWN RADIO STATION

In some countries, the licensing authority allows organizations, including churches, to run special-event or restricted service stations which operate like ordinary FM stations for a short time, and on restricted power. These can be an exciting feature for a mission or festival which can reach large numbers of people, can involve the whole community in the mission or festival and can cost as little as a few thousand pounds. A number of trusts will make grants available to enable churches to set up small, special-event radio stations, and equipment is sometimes available.

Running a radio station, even for a day or so, takes an enormous amount of planning and not a little finance, so it pays to start early and plan well. But it can have a huge impact, and be great fun for those involved. Try to draw together a small team who will each take on one aspect of the station:

◆ a general manager to co-ordinate the team

◆ someone to look after equipment provision, technical matters and licensing

◆ someone to develop the programming

◆ someone to develop links with the community

◆ someone to look after the music, and provide a suitable record library and play list

◆ someone to raise the money

Often a local church will provide suitable temporary accommodation for the studio and a production room, and Christians working in journalism can be co-opted to help with the programming. It doesn't have to be on air for twenty-four hours a day, but some authorities require a 'sustaining signal' to be broadcast during the time that the station is not operating, so that the frequency remains occupied.

USING THE RELIGIOUS PROGRAMMES

Religious programmes on radio have a specific audience, and it is not always correct to assume that only the religious programme will be interested in your news. Always consider whether your story is of general interest, and if so, send it first to the news editor. It makes the point that you think your story is of general interest, and some journalists need to be shown that religious news is interesting to the general listener, as well as to the religious producer. After all, in the UK there are more members of Christian churches than there are of political parties! You can always copy your news release to the religious producer.

However, the religious programme has a special function. It speaks to those who are interested in religious matters, those who are unable to go to church, and those who 'belong' either by attending or by association. It is the 'trade press', and can go deeper into an issue, using language and thought patterns that are understood by church people. Again, it depends on who you want to reach. If you want to speak to the religious or Christian community in the station's editorial area, then the religious programme is the place to aim for. But if you want to speak to the community at large, you should try to get your story in through the news desk.

THE BREAKFAST/LUNCH/DRIVE-TIME SHOW

These are the radio equivalent to the newspapers' short features. If your story doesn't make the news, it might be interesting to the producer of the breakfast programme, or the lunch-time show, or the programme run mainly for people driving home from work. Try to discover the name of the producers of these programmes, and give them a ring. This can often result in some considerable publicity, or even a special feature.

Radio is an extremely effective medium to choose for personal communication. Remember: even though there may be thousands of listeners, you are broadcasting to a single listener, not addressing a mass audience. And thanks to the gift of imagination, the pictures are much better!

NEWSPAPERS AS A MEDIUM 17

There is an enormous range of newspapers and magazines published in most countries, and they can be roughly divided into the following types:

◆ international daily newspapers

◆ national daily newspapers

◆ national Sunday newspapers

◆ regional daily newspapers

◆ local weekly newspapers

◆ local free papers

◆ specialist trade newspapers

◆ hobby and leisure magazines

◆ women's interest magazines

◆ consumer magazines

◆ specialist and trade magazines.

Of the printed and broadcast media, it is claimed by some that television has the greatest influence. Certainly it has the largest audience. In Britain, ninety-eight per cent of households have a television set and the owners spend an average of twenty-five hours a week watching them. An audience in excess of twenty million has been recorded for some television programmes in the UK.

In terms of size, radio comes second, with the average British householder listening to radio for more than fifteen hours a week.

Figures published by RAJAR (Radio Joint Audience Research Limited) show the following:

ILR (76 stations, 105 services)	31.2%
BBC Radio 1	22.4%
BBC Radio 2	13.0%
BBC Radio 4	10.8%
BBC Local Radio (38 local radio stations)	9.5%
Classic FM	2.8%
BBC Radio 3	1.3%
Others	7.7%

Although newspapers come a poor third in terms of readers when compared with the viewers and listeners to television and radio, they still wield an influence which is considerably larger than their circulation might indicate. It only takes one major newspaper to run a major story for it to be picked up by the other media. But the number of times a major story is broken by television, and certainly by radio, is considerably smaller.

Circulation figures for daily newspapers (Audit Bureau of Circulations 1992) are as follows (figures in millions):

Sun	3.63
Daily Mirror	2.83
Daily Mail	1.74
Daily Express	1.56
Daily Telegraph	1.04
Daily Star	0.81
Today	0.536
Guardian	0.414
The Times	0.377
Independent	0.375
Financial Times	0.289

Circulation figures for Sunday newspapers (Audit Bureau of Circulations 1992) are:

News of the World	4.79
Sunday Mirror	2.74
People	2.11
Mail on Sunday	1.97
Sunday Express	1.80
The Sunday Times	1.18
Sunday Telegraph	0.59
Observer	0.527
Independent on Sunday	0.417

To understand why circulation figures like this should give a greater proportional influence than radio or television, we need to understand three important things about the medium.

First, it is easier to refer back to a story printed in a newspaper than it is to a story broadcast on radio or television. You only have to open the paper, and the story is there, hour after hour, day after day. You can cut it out and paste it into a cuttings book, where it can easily be read. You can read it, and re-read it; you can refer back to it as many times as you like. And, compared with radio and television, the story can be written in considerable depth.

Compare this with a story which is broadcast on radio or television, which is gone within seconds. The only way to capture it is by means of tape or hard disk. It is, by nature of the medium, here one moment, gone the next.

Secondly, newspapers tend to employ more journalists, and certainly more specialized journalists, than either radio or television. This means that they can spend more time searching for news, and more time following up leads. They can be out and about in the community, whereas their television and radio counterparts tend to work from their studios, following up stories fed to them by specialist news agencies, who in turn often get their stories from the newspapers!

Thirdly, newspapers are targeted at particular socio-economic groups. This means that those newspapers which are targeted at the decision makers are going to have a major influence on the life of the nation. For example, London's *Evening Standard*, read on the way home from London by over half a million people including civil servants, leaders and politicians, precedes the early evening news on television, and sets the scene for both the evening and the following day's news.

USING NEWSPAPERS

The local newspaper is the first place that most church communicators turn to when they want to get their story out. It is a good place to start, but not necessarily the only place. There are a number of things you need to know about your local newspaper before you make a final decision about its suitability for your purpose:

◆ its editorial area

◆ its circulation figures

◆ its publication day

◆ its editorial deadline

◆ whether it is daily, weekly or freesheet.

Having found these things out, you can then consider how best to use the newspaper. Do you want to send in a news story? Or is the subject matter more suitable for a longer feature? Is what you are sending in a genuine news story (which may well be used) or are you really asking for free advertising (which probably will not)? Are you able to meet the editorial deadline for publication, or will your news story be history by the next publication date? (If your local newspaper is a weekly, and you've just missed the editorial deadline, why not consider the local radio station? The access is immediate, and if your story is strong enough, it could be out within the next couple of hours!)

There is no better way to understand your local newspaper than to take it regularly, and to read it. You will begin to get a 'feel' for the kind of stories it favours, and you will be better equipped to persuade the news or features editor to take your stories.

In addition to news stories, there are several other ways of using your local or regional newspaper:

◆ write a 'letter to the editor'

◆ try to get a picture story

◆ use the 'what's on' diary

◆ interest the features editor in a possible feature

◆ take out advertising.

WRITING A LETTER TO THE EDITOR

There are a number of reasons for writing a letter for publication:

◆ correcting an inaccurate article or news story

◆ raising an issue of public concern

◆ putting a different point of view on a current topic

◆ giving information about your organization

◆ campaigning for an issue or organization

◆ saying 'thank you' after an event.

As in all things, knowing the rules and using them gives you a greater chance of success. The letters editor may have a large number of letters from which to choose, and yours may not be one of them.

◆ Decide on the one or two main points you want to make.

◆ Write legibly, or preferably type.

◆ Don't be afraid of controversy or humour.

◆ Keep your letter as brief as possible

◆ Don't write too often!

Where you are writing to correct an inaccuracy, do so straight away, with good grace, and if possible, with a touch of humour.

THE PICTURE STORY

Sometimes, a picture is all that is needed to tell a story. Most newspapers run 'picture stories', and where you think a picture might be a good idea, the following needs to be done:

◆ Write out your news release, giving the five 'w's about the picture opportunity (see page 73).

◆ Telephone the newspaper and ask for the picture desk.

◆ Explain your picture story, and then send the picture desk your news release.

Picture stories can be a great help in keeping your church in the news, and are a good way of illustrating an event.

USING THE DIARIES

Most newspapers keep two sorts of diaries. The first kind is used by the news editor and the picture editor to decide where to send journalists and photographers that day. It contains all the things that are happening in their editorial area for the day that they know of, so it's important for your event to be in the diary if it's to stand any chance of being covered. This kind of diary is organizational, and not for publication.

Let the newspaper know in good time of events that are planned well in advance, and they will go in the diary. Then when the news editor or picture editor looks at the deployment of their staff for that day, they will at least consider your event as a possibility. You have to be 'in' to win!

The other kind of diary is the 'what's on' diary for the area, and is for publication. Many local newspapers publish a considerable number of 'what's on's free of charge, and it can be a popular feature which gains readers. If you want your event to go in the published 'what's on', then make it clear in your letter. Most newspapers refuse to accept 'what's on' events over the telephone, because of the danger of mistakes.

TRY FOR A FEATURE

Features are usually an in-depth account centred on a person, an event or a place. They are put together much further in advance than the news story—often as much as three or four weeks—and can be as long as a full page. They are a most valuable way of raising the profile of your church or organization. Most newspapers spend a great deal of time and energy on their features, and work with the picture editor to get really interesting pictures.

If you think a feature is an appropriate response to an event or an issue, the first thing to do is to telephone the newspaper and ask to speak to the features editor. Suggest the possibility and discuss it, but make sure you have all the facts to hand before you do. Most features editors are glad to have suggestions and, although they may not respond, at least you will have tried.

TAKE OUT ADVERTISING

We all get tired of people who continually want something for nothing, and there's no reason why newspaper editors should feel any differently about the church that always asks for free publicity for their events. The main income stream for most newspapers is from their advertising, and we need to look carefully at the stories we are sending in. Are they really only asking for free advertising of an event? If so, why not take out an advertisement?

Advertising rates are published by all

newspapers, and are available from advertising sales departments. Costs vary, depending on the size of your proposed advertisement and the circulation of the particular newspaper. You can either opt for a display advertisement, which gives you space to be a bit creative, or a classified advertisement, which is usually cheaper, but not so prominent.

The other advantage about taking advertising space is that it does act as an incentive for the newspaper to support your event.

Do beware, however, of the persuasive advertising sales executive on the free newspaper. Free newspapers are there to make money from their advertising sales, and no matter what they might say, most of them put sales income first and journalism second. If someone contacts you to sell advertising, apply the following filters:

◆ Is the paper's readership in my target group?

◆ Is the cost justified?

◆ Is the advertisement likely to have the suggested effect?

And give yourself time to think about the proposal. Never agree to an advertisement on the first contact.

THE TRADE PRESS

Many newspapers are published not for general circulation, but for specific interest groups. Here's a sample of a few trade titles that are published every week, taken at random from one of the media directories (PIMS Media Directory), with their circulation (in thousands):

The Tax Journal	**12**
Farmers' Weekly	**98**
Business in Essex Daily	**32**
General Practitioner	**42**
Gardening News	**114**
British Baker	**10**
Amateur Photographer	**55**

There are many more monthly and quarterly papers and magazines on just about every topic that you can possibly think of. How about *Paintball Games Magazine* (circulation 20,000), or *Doll's House World* (circulation 15,000)?

If you have a good story, it pays to think laterally. What trade press might be interested in this? The choir member who has just completed 40 years in the choir happens to be a leading member of Rotary, so how about sending the story, with a photograph, to the Rotary magazine (circulation 64,000)? Or the new church building that has just been announced? How about sending the story to *Church Building* (circulation 9,000)?

USING MEDIA DIRECTORIES

Media directories are an invaluable tool for the church communicator. In the UK, for example, there are a number of media directories ranging from annual publications that can be bought from a bookshop for a few pounds, to a computer listing which is updated daily and available to subscribers via a computer link. These more complex listings usually cost a considerable sum of money, but there are many ways that a church communicator can gain access to a media listing:

- through their church's central communications office
- through the local reference library
- through a public relations agency.

PIMS is probably the UK's leading media listing. Its main publications include a quarterly directory listing every publication, radio and television programme in the UK grouped under topic headings, together with their circulation, and the names of all the specialist journalists with their phone and fax numbers; a quarterly town list, listing all the media outlets (newspapers, radio and television) available by town; a business directory; a European directory; and a USA directory. The PIMS computer can be accessed direct via a modem link, and data downloaded to give specific mailing lists, together with data to create the labels! The service is not cheap, but it is comprehensive.

THE INTERNAL BULLETIN AND HOUSE JOURNAL

Most large organizations, including major companies and service institutions, run a house journal for employees, and many smaller companies have an internal bulletin. These can be a superb means of communication, although discovering their points of access can be a little time-consuming. Special-interest groups are usually networked through some kind of newsletter, and these too can provide a highly focused market for your story or information.

When dealing with newsprint, think creatively, and think laterally. Don't be content simply with putting your story in the parish magazine. Let it speak to the whole community.

DEALING WITH BAD NEWS 18

There are times when the church, or someone in it, gets into the news without any effort on the part of the press officer or communicator. Things can, and do, go wrong, and the media are quick to follow a story that interests people. There are two kinds of 'bad news':

◆ where the church is incidental to the story (for example, a funeral for disaster victims)

◆ where the church is the source of the story (for example, a clergyman who misbehaves).

In both cases, the task of the communicator is

◆ by establishing clear boundaries, to create a space where the church can get on with its task of mission and pastoral care without undue interference from the media

◆ to act as a gatekeeper, feeding appropriate information to the media, and allowing them to do their job without creating undue interference to the church.

REMEMBER YOUR THEOLOGY

When these pressures strike, as they will inevitably do from time to time, it helps to remember the theological framework within which we operate. We live in a fallen world, but Jesus did not come to condemn it. He came because he loved it, and wanted to heal and restore it. Yet that healing love was rejected, and the world called for his crucifixion. How much more, then, should we expect the world to want to crucify us in words and pictures when we fail? Our job is to remain open and vulnerable, protecting others whilst laying ourselves open to question.

PLANNING FOR CRISIS

Every organization, including the local church, should have some kind of plan for when a crisis strikes. At its simplest, a crisis plan is a checklist of who to contact and what to do if certain events happen. There is no substitute for practising, and no crisis plan can be called a plan until it has been exercised at least once. Most people suffer from some kind of shock when things happen which are out of the ordinary, and a carefully prepared and rehearsed plan can help them respond effectively.

The following checklist is provided for a major problem, but the principles behind it can be applied in almost every minor crisis.

NOMINATE A CRISIS RESPONSE TEAM

There need to be three key people in the crisis response team:

◆ the communicator

◆ the manager

◆ the expert.

They each need to know who the others are. The task of the communicator is to advise on information flow and handle the media; the task of the manager is to manage the situation, and the task of the expert is to provide expert advice on the cause, effect and handling of the crisis. All three need to be available to the printed and broadcast media.

ESTABLISH THE FACTS

At first, the facts will be partial, confused, and difficult to obtain. The team needs to write down in a short statement:

◆ what they know as fact

◆ what might have happened

◆ what immediate action they can take

◆ where the press point is to be established.

PREPARE AN INITIAL STATEMENT

The communicator will be under pressure from the media to respond. If the incident is a major one, he or she should hold a brief news conference at the press point, where the manager (if possible), or the communicator (where the manager is too busy) should say:

◆ what they know has happened

◆ what they are doing to mitigate the effects

◆ how sorry they are for what has happened

◆ when they might be able to give further information.

At that initial news conference, the expert should be available to be questioned on possible cause, possible effect, and means of mitigation. There are three golden rules which must be followed:

◆ never lie

◆ never try to hide what has happened

◆ always express sorrow where harm has been done.

MAINTAIN THE APPROPRIATE BOUNDARIES

The journalist's job is to get as much information, including pictures, as possible. And the communicator's job is to protect those working on the crisis from undue interference from the media. There needs to be a clear boundary between the media and the incident, together with appropriate ways of feeding information across the boundary. The crisis team needs to know what the media are asking, and the media need to know what the crisis team are doing.

People at the centre of a problem need to be protected. They may be physically or emotionally damaged, and they may need to be taken to a place where they can be physically or emotionally cared for. This is as true for a small, local difficulty as it is for a major incident. Families, relatives and those in shock need to be protected. A neighbour or friend should answer the door or the telephone for them, so that they are not put in the position of being unable to avoid answering questions or having their photographs taken.

The team may need to locate a 'safe house' where emotionally damaged people can be protected from the attention of the media and where they can be supported by people who are sympathetic to their plight. There is always a real danger of self-inflicted harm where individuals are left unsupported and exposed to continuous media pressure, and the crisis manager should always have this in mind when dealing with people under severe pressure.

The press point is the gateway between the media and those directly involved in a problem, and I have found that it helps to think of the boundaries in almost physical or geographical terms. Where pictures are needed, the photographers can nominate one of their number to act on a rota basis, supplying pictures to the others. The nominated photographer can be accompanied across the boundary on the understanding that he or she will leave if asked.

MAINTAIN THE INFORMATION FLOW

At first, journalists will need basic information for their news reports, together with any photographs that might be possible. But as time passes, they will need other information for features, in-depth analysis, and documentary-style reports.

Where funerals or memorials are taking place, several things will be needed:

◆ the names of all those taking part, and their position in the hierarchy

◆ copies of the order of service

◆ copies of the funeral or memorial address

◆ the names of any mourners of political or other newsworthy significance.

WHEN AND HOW TO SAY NOTHING

There are very few times when it is best practice to say nothing. Even in the middle of a bad or embarrassing story, or probably especially then, a journalist's request for a statement will give you the opportunity to put your side of the argument, or to mitigate the embarrassment. But there are times when saying nothing is not only the best policy but the right course of action:

◆ where matters are subject to the *sub judice* rule

◆ where matters relate to a private relationship between an employer and employee

◆ where matters are personal to an individual and you have not got that individual's permission to comment.

In all these cases, never say, 'No comment'. Always explain why you are not making any comment on that particular matter, and stick to your position. Although the journalist might push you a bit, most will respect your integrity in the end. It is better to say something like, 'We do not comment on matters that are private between an employer and an employee.' Most journalists will respect this, even if they push you a bit. After all, if they were in the same situation, they wouldn't like their private lives exposed for scrutiny.

Bad news needs to be handled by someone with a clear head and strong nerves. Beware of appointing someone as a crisis manager or communicator who has had their own personal crisis within the previous three years.

POSTERS AND LEAFLETS 19

POSTERS

Posters are attention-grabbers. The picture, line drawing or logo acts as a hook, and the poster can be targeted fairly precisely at different groups of people by the use of appropriate images. The words convey basic information, and point beyond themselves, either to where more information can be obtained, or to where an event is taking place.

Posters come in all shapes and sizes, from the small A5 poster designed for a crowded notice-board to the forty foot by ten foot ninety-sheet outdoor poster. The more common twenty foot by ten foot outdoor poster is used by industry and commerce as a prime advertising size, and selling poster space at this level is a major industry.

Posters are used to advertise events, to advertise products, to challenge assumptions, to give information, and to entertain. They can be used singly, or in large numbers to create a cumulative effect.

Posters cannot convey large amounts of information, and the smaller sizes are not good at conveying complex arguments. They work best conveying one single carefully targeted message using a 'visual' that hooks the people that message is intended for.

There are six elements to a poster campaign:

◆ the size and number displayed
◆ the picture or 'visual'
◆ the words
◆ the positioning
◆ the production
◆ the distribution.

SIZE AND NUMBER DISPLAYED

What is your poster for? If it is for school notice-boards, then sizes above A4, or A3 at the most, will not be used. If it's for church notice-boards, then A4 is a good size. If it is a campaign designed to reach the motorist, then at least a four-sheet, if not a forty-eight-sheet, is needed. What about putting your poster on a bus, or on a train? Would it be more effective on a bus-stop? Or at the local railway station?

PICTURES OR 'VISUALS'

Most posters are seen by hundreds of different people, of all ages, professions and interests. Yet most carry a message that is designed to reach one particular group of people. The thing that targets the poster at these people, that 'hooks' them into hearing the message, is the picture or visual representation.

For example, suppose a poster is designed to carry a message for people interested in sea fishing. One way of hooking this group is to put a picture of an expensive sea-fishing rod, and a good-sized sea fish, such as a conger eel or a large cod, as your visual. Those people who are interested in sea fishing will at least try to identify the rod, or the fish, and will read the message at the same time.

Or, as another example, suppose a poster is designed to carry a message for parents with young children. There are several symbols of young parenthood that could be used: the nappy, the feeding bottle, the buggy or the safety gate. Any of these symbols could be used to attract attention.

If your budget does not stretch to a full-colour picture, you can always use line drawings. If these are stylized in an attractive way, they can enhance both the 'hook' and the message considerably.

THE WORDS

There need to be as few words as possible, designed to blend with the visual, but not to be obscured or dominated by it. The message needs to be crisp and clear. Remember the lessons of the communications plan: be clear about the response you want.

Humour is always a good tool, but it needs to be carefully handled. Religious words, on the other hand, are usually not a good idea. 'Have you been washed by the Blood?' is not perhaps the best way to advertise a church, whereas the question, 'When did you last say "Thanks"?', alongside a stylized line drawing of a church, or even a stylized line drawing of a figure on a cross, might be.

THE POSITIONING

Posters need to be placed where their target audience has a chance of seeing them. This might sound obvious, but large numbers of outreach posters get no further than the church noticeboard. Often, prime sites are available at some cost, and it is worth considering paying for sites if the main thrust of your campaign is through posters. Many poster site companies operate a discount scheme for charities, giving spare sites to charities at low cost, and provided the timings fit your campaign, these are certainly worth considering.

POSTER PRODUCTION

Most posters can be printed by any commercial printers, but it is worth getting quotations from specialist poster printers, particularly if you are using four-sheet size or above as these really require poster paper which has a special backing. Printers that buy this in bulk are likely to give a lower quotation than a high-street printer who would have to buy it in specially.

DISTRIBUTION

If you are booking a number of sites from a specialist poster site owner (such as Maiden Outdoor in the UK) the distribution and posting is included in the cost. Where the campaign is smaller, and you are relying on volunteer helpers, it is useful to produce a guidance sheet for posting, which gives ideas about where to post, and equally, prevents the over-enthusiastic from posting your campaign in places where it will discredit the message. Many churches will be able to provide volunteers for distribution and posting, and the notes of guidance should include a target date for posting, so that the posters all go up on, or near, the same date.

POSTER USE

Posters can be used in conjunction with other elements of a campaign, and are especially useful when combined with leaflets. The poster can give the core message, and the leaflet, which carries the same visual, can go into greater detail, and can even carry some form of response coupon.

LEAFLETS

Leaflets can either be used as a free 'pick-up' item, or can be delivered in various ways to targeted groups of people. They can carry a picture 'hook'; a core message on the cover; detailed information on the inside; and a response coupon with either a business reply or freepost address.

The design of a leaflet requires specialist design skills, but essentially it needs to have the same 'hook' as a poster: the design, pictures and line drawings need to 'hook' into the target group that the leaflet is aimed at.

Leaflets can range in size and complexity from the A5 handbill (with or without clip coupon), to the glossy eight-page mini-brochure. Leaflets go well with a poster campaign: they can be used in a mailshot, and they can be placed in strategic places as a casual 'pick-up' from desks, counters, shops and libraries—in fact, anywhere where people congregate.

Although you can put forward a complex argument, or a number of mini statements, the leaflet needs to have one clear communication aim. Leaflets work by taking the reader from this one clearly defined message through a series of steps to a conclusion. They might be used to present a diary of events at a festival, or to explain the baptism policy of a local church. They might be given away free in the shops as part of a campaign, or posted to people on a carefully selected mailing list.

But both the design and the distribution of the leaflet need to reflect its purpose. Its no good producing a glossy eight-page leaflet in an expensive format with a complex argument about, say, an appeal to preserve the architecture of a building, and then giving the leaflet away to casual shoppers in the local marketplace. Many of them will end up on the street, being walked over and muddied by uninterested shoppers, and the message of care and quality will be damaged, if not entirely lost.

Given the Christian commitment to ecology and the care of created resources, it is important to consider how the leaflet is going to be distributed. Only print the number of leaflets that you calculate you are going to use, and try to distribute them in a way that avoids waste. Street handouts are never a good way of using leaflets, unless they contain a free offer, or some other 'hook' which encourages people not to throw them on the street.

If you intend to use the leaflet for a major campaign, try to get quotations from a few designers. Look at their portfolios, and see which have the right 'feel' for the job. If you're using posters and leaflets combined, try to use the same designer for both, and see if the quotation can include both items. Once the leaflet has been designed, the amount of work to put the picture and words on the poster is often minor (and if the poster has been designed, this is also true for the leaflet).

20 THE CHURCH MAGAZINE

The church or 'parish' magazine is almost an institution in some churches. It may well have been there since the last century, published every month, and delivered by generations of dedicated volunteers. The average parish magazine, if it has a cover price and is not a free-distribution paper, has a circulation roughly 2.8 times the membership roll of the church (a calculation that rarely fails). Its readership can be defined fairly closely: the core membership of the church, plus those who belong 'by association', rather than by regular attendance.

The communication aim of most church magazines is simply to remind people that the church is there. It goes out, month after month, with the minister's letter, the various rotas, sometimes a children's page (though the number of children who read it is usually small), and a range of articles either home-grown, or culled from syndicated support material or other sources.

There is usually an editor, appointed by the church (or more often, persuaded by the minister), whose job it is to produce the goods every month. Yet rarely is the magazine discussed by the church committee, and even more rarely is it really 'owned' by the church leadership.

Yet the magazine is a fairly central communication platform, and for some churches, it is the only communication platform. Even if the magazine were not read, the simple act of putting it through the letterboxes of several hundred people each month gives them a clear message: you belong! So whose magazine is it? Does it belong to the minister, who (perhaps) has the veto over what goes in and what is left out? Does it belong to the editor, whose job it is to put it together each month? Does it belong to the church, whose life and ministry is reflected in its pages? Or does it belong to the local community, who pay for it each month?

For the church magazine to be successful, rather than simply 'there', it does need to be owned by the church and the church committee. This means taking care to support the editor and the editorial team, and working out the precise relationship between editorial freedom and church (or ministerial) control. But most of all it means having a clear, and agreed, communication aim.

DEFINING THE COMMUNICATION AIM

There are three broad groups of people that the magazine might be designed to reach:

◆ church members (those who belong by 'participation')

◆ fringe members (those who belong by 'association')

◆ those who don't (yet) associate or participate

You can think of these three groups on a sliding scale, and draw a chart showing exactly where the magazine is intended to sit. For example, its aim might be to keep core members informed. If this is the case, its content will be about issues and concerns at the heart of running and developing the church and its ministry. It will be an 'insider's' magazine.

It's more likely that core members will be kept informed by other means; by minutes, or by team meetings, or even by telephone. In which case, the magazine might be aimed at those who belong, either by participation or by association. Its content, production and distribution will reflect this, and it will probably have a cover price and a subscription list.

Or it might be aimed partly at those who belong by association, and partly at those who don't belong at all. Its content will reflect its aim, and it might well be distributed free on a regular basis.

Or it might be aimed at those completely outside the church. If this is the case, its content is likely to be lighter, its format possibly A3 folded to make a four-page A4 leaflet (A4 fly) with plenty of pictures, and its distribution less frequent (two or three times a year, linked with major festivals).

The magazine should be an integral part of the church's communications plan, with a clearly defined and agreed communication aim integrated with the other parts of the plan. There is nothing to prevent a church publishing documents with different aims at different times of the year:

◆ a free, four-page newsletter (A3 folded to four pages of A4) with lots of pictures and easy-to-read text, distributed free to every home at Christmas, Mothering Sunday/Easter, and Harvest Festival (or other suitable times)

◆ a magazine with cover price and subscription list published nine times a year aimed at those who belong 'by association'.

◆ a weekly 'notice sheet' distributed free in church, aimed at keeping core members informed of committee discussions, mission plans, etc.

The free distribution sheet could be aimed at gaining both visitors to the key visitors' services, and at gaining subscribers to the magazine. It could have a freepost clip coupon for potential subscribers, or for other Christian literature, or even for requests for a visit from the minister.

RUNNING THE MAGAZINE/ NEWSLETTER

There are six separate operations needed to run a successful magazine:

◆ finding the right editorial material

◆ editing the material

◆ layout and design of the cover and pages

◆ printing and production

◆ distribution

◆ finance and administration.

FINDING THE RIGHT EDITORIAL MATERIAL

Any editor will tell you that the first thing they learned was that the material didn't just come to them—they had to go out and commission it. And persuading people to write for the parish magazine is fraught with difficulties. There are those who simply refuse, and those who take a lot of persuading. There are those who cannot keep to your deadline. Then there are those who threaten to leave the church if you so much as alter a single word, and there are those rare and beautiful people who agree to write on a topic, and produce it, neatly typed, before the deadline has expired!

Sources of material for the church magazine include:

◆ commissioned articles from members

◆ commissioned articles from non-members

◆ children's art and stories

◆ syndicated material (commercially available) such as the Church News Service

◆ extracts from missionary societies' leaflets

◆ extracts from other Christian groups' leaflets (they are usually delighted for you to reprint their material, as long as you acknowledge the source)

◆ material produced by children from the local school

◆ local walks and byways (ask an enthusiast)

◆ local history, including the history of the church (ask another enthusiast)

◆ the minister's letter

◆ issue of the month (ask some of the younger members to contribute to this)

◆ features on twin towns, or twin churches overseas

◆ features on interesting people in the community (a very popular item, this, but with hidden dangers)

◆ those rotas necessary to prevent the church coming to a complete standstill.

The list could go on. Get the magazine team to brainstorm one evening, and write down all their ideas of where material could come from.

Given that people sometimes fail to work to deadlines, it is possible to work more than one edition in advance. News, obviously, has to be fresh. But features can be commissioned for two or three editions in advance, and edited in spare moments.

EDITING THE MATERIAL

Editing is done for a number of reasons:

◆ to make the material more easily understood

◆ to make the material fit a limited space

◆ to clarify tortuous, long or convoluted writing

◆ to remove superfluous words.

It helps the editing process if, when people are asked to produce an article, it is on the understanding that the editor reserves the right to cut or edit the article to the required length. The editor can always check the edited piece with its author, and a good editor will be able to sub-edit a piece so well that the writer will hardly notice what has been done, but goes away thinking, 'I did write that well!'

Editing is a skill that requires practice, but after a while it can be done fairly quickly. Editing on a word-processor is even quicker, and if contributors can give their work on disk, it saves re-keying the article.

The acid test of all editing, and of all editorial relationships, is when the vicar or minister's letter needs to be cut. There is absolutely no reason why the minister's letter should not be treated in the same way as anyone else's article. Abstruse, complicated language from the minister will lose readers just as quickly as from anyone else, and provided the final copy is checked with the minister, an edited letter can be much more effective!

Here is a short article contributed by one of the bellringers at a local church.

Notwithstanding the decline in church attendance which I've seen with my own eyes since I was a lad, we still get lots of people coming along to ring the bells. All sorts of people climb the spiral stone staircase to the ringing chamber each week. There's Bob Harris, the local butcher, and Michael Sanders who runs his own company. Mary Jones has been ringing the bells since she came as a teacher to the village school nearly 27 years ago, and Steven Prabble who is nearly sixteen, and lives down the road from the church where he heard the bells ringing and thought to himself, 'I'd like to do that', so he came along, and Bill Wilde, who used to be Church Treasurer, but gave up because he didn't like the way the Diocese asked him to present the accounts.

Ringing is great fun, and each Sunday we meet at 10.00 o'clock ready to ring for the 10.30 service. We have a ring of six bells, so we need six people each week to make up a band. We don't do too badly, though there was a time when we were a bit short, and Bill tried to ring two bells at the same time, and got his timing wrong. The Vicar said it was just like the war!

If anyone would like to join us, we practise on Thursday evenings. Just come along to the tower. We'd love to see you.

The article is 244 words, and too long for the space. So this is how it was edited. You may be able to suggest better ways:

Not so many people come to church these days, but we still get lots of people coming along to ring the bells. All sorts climb the spiral stone staircase to the ringing chamber each week. There's Bob Harris, the local butcher, and Michael Sanders who runs his own company. Mary Jones has been ringing the bells since she came to the village school nearly twenty-seven years ago, and Steven Prabble who is nearly sixteen, heard the bells ringing from his home, thought to himself, 'I'd like to do that', and just came along. Then there's Bill Wilde, who used to be church treasurer, and who once tried to ring two bells at the same time when we were short of ringers, and got his timing wrong.

Ringing is great fun. We meet at 10.00 a.m. each Sunday to ring for the 10.30 service, and practise on Thursday evenings. If you'd like to join us, just come along to the tower. We'd love to see you.

The article now has only 167 words (a reduction of 31%), fits the space, and has had some of the more difficult wrinkles smoothed out. And hopefully, it has kept its original 'feel'.

LAYOUT AND DESIGN

There are three golden rules for good layout:

◆ make sure there's plenty of white space on the page

◆ don't use more than two typefaces

◆ keep the same 'shape' so that people know where they are each month.

Pictures can be an enormous help, can break up the page, and can provide stories all by themselves. It's not difficult these days to incorporate photographs into a church magazine. Artwork can help, too, especially if the children are encouraged to contribute. There is nothing better than seeing children's art featured regularly in the church magazine, together with the names and ages of the children who contributed.

There is a wealth of clip-art available today, commercially produced to 'fill' the odd space, and to provide signposts to the various types of article. But beware: it doesn't take much to overdo it, and the magazine turns from a quiet, well-laid-out production to a cluttered, messy one. Here's a tip: get local children to produce the symbols you need, and use them on a regular basis.

PRINTING AND PRODUCTION

There are a number of options for printing and production, depending on circulation size, budget and volunteer strength.

Duplication

Thankfully, this method is disappearing fast, because it is a messy, rather dull reproduction process that is almost impossible to use for artwork and photographs.

Photocopying

Excellent for short runs, and for including children's art and line drawings, but not so good for photographs (unless they are screened), and expensive where large runs are required. Despite advances in technology, photocopiers are renowned for going wrong, and should always have a service contract with them. There are some sharks around in the photocopying leasing business, so buyer beware.

Offset litho printing

If the church can afford (or can share the cost) of an offset litho printer, it can be an enormous boon. These are great for reproducing everything from text and line drawings to (screened) photographs. Paper plates can be made on many photocopiers, and the machine can be made to earn its keep by printing odd jobs for church members. One disadvantage is that sizes above A4 are very expensive to produce, and you will need larger plate-making equipment. It's also a potentially messy process, and it's important to keep everything clean, so a water supply and a sink is needed. It can also be quite difficult at first to learn the process.

Copy printing

A version of the offset litho which makes its own plates and disposes of its own waste. (It doesn't write the magazine, though!)

Commercial printing

Excellent if you have the budget, but it can lose the community atmosphere of volunteers collating, folding and stapling each month.

After the printing process is complete, there is still the business of collating the magazine, folding it and stapling it. There are commercially produced folding machines, though you will need to allow for at least ten per cent wastage in these, and a saddle-back electric stapler can save fingers and misfires!

USING PHOTOGRAPHS

Photographs convey information, feelings, and stories. They make a magazine more readable. People like looking at photographs. But getting them into a low-budget magazine isn't easy. Find someone to take good photographs for you, preferably in black and white, and get the photographs 'screened' so that thay can be reproduced more clearly when photocopied or printed. A screened photograph is made up of hundreds of tiny dots, all of different intensities. (You can see the dots through a magnifying glass, e.g. in black and white photographs in a newspaper.)

DISTRIBUTION

The type of distribution you choose depends largely on the communication aim of the magazine. There are two traditional methods:

- ◆ distribution to subscribers who pay a cover price

- ◆ free distribution to a whole community

Distribution to a subscribers' list usually involves a team of magazine distributors, faithful people who help support the ministry of the church by taking a few magazines each month to individual subscribers. It's also a way for church members to keep in touch with those who may not come regularly, or at all, either through disability, age, or the fact that they only belong by association.

Free distribution can be achieved by one of several methods:

- ◆ Using church members to distribute in their own locality. This involves keeping quite a good administration process if the whole area is to be covered, and some church members are not to be given proportionally bigger tasks than others. It can only be done a few times a year.

- ◆ Using a local free newspaper to deliver the leaflets with their paper. This has the advantage that it avoids burdening the church members, but the disadvantage that it costs money, and can also be 'patchy' because many people refuse to accept 'free' newspapers.

- Using the Post Office to deliver the leaflets with the mail. This is a very accurate and effective method, but it is very expensive.

- Using a local marketing firm to deliver. In many large towns, there are local marketing firms who will employ their own delivery staff, and they will be pleased to quote for a precisely targeted delivery of leaflets.

If you are starting off from scratch, and want to build a subscribers' list, there are several methods that can be used, alone or combined:

- a leaflet with a clip coupon distributed free to every house, coupled with a launch in the local press

- a free magazine to every resident in each street, followed by a visit by the distributor a week later (this can be a staggered approach to build a small list into a bigger one)

- copies sold in local shops, but each copy containing an order form for regular subscription.

FINANCING THE MAGAZINE

In the first section of the book we looked at resources, and suggested that the best results are achieved when identified and agreed resources are deployed against clearly defined communication aims. The financial resources for a publication can come from:

- subscription income
- the communication budget of the church
- advertising income
- sponsorship
- a combination of the above.

The worst form of resourcing is when neither the magazine editor or team, nor the church council, really know how much the magazine is costing, but 'it's doing a good job, so we pay for it.' That may be fine from the viewpoint of the church council or elders, but it doesn't give the magazine team much incentive to improve its efficiency, or any confidence to use surplus income to develop the publication. How often have we heard magazine editors say something like, 'I'd love to do this or that, but I don't know if we have the money.'

If the magazine, or free leaflet, or whatever the publication is, has its own budget, with any subsidy from the church clearly identified as a separate item, then the editor and his or her team have the incentive to become more efficient, to experiment by using funds in different ways, and to make a case to the church for increased subsidies for specific projects where these are proposed. This in turn helps the church to discuss and own the aims of the magazine. The editor and the team feel that they are more a part of the mission and ministry of the church, and everyone benefits.

Equally, where the budget is separately defined, it may identify surplus income which can either be given back to the church for specific mission activity, or ploughed back into the publication for its development. Either way, the magazine team's morale will improve, even if the separation of the budget identifies a considerable 'loss' which the church then agrees is the cost of that particular bit of their mission.

Subscription income

This can come from a cover price collected at point of sale or delivery, or from an annual subscription by the readers. It needs to be set at a realistic market price, but if increases are needed, they probably need to be phased over several years. The cover price is usually a sensitive issue with people who belong 'by association', and it is easy to lose subscribers by increasing the cover price too speedily. Setting a cover price gives the magazine a value, and can increase the respect with which it is received. It can also bring in a considerable sum. For example:

Cover Price:	**£0.35**
Total copies:	**4,200**
Total income:	**£1,470**

The communication budget of the church

If the editor or magazine team are not members of the church council, deacons' meeting, or elders, they could be invited once a year to discuss the aims of the magazine, and the level of subsidy. This can help the church as a whole develop its communication policy, and should be done in such a way as to help the editor and magazine team feel part of the wider ministry and mission of the church.

If the church does not have a communication budget, it could be a specific item from the general fund. Where this doesn't exist at present, it can be an excellent move to propose that the subsidy be identified, quantified, debated and owned by the church. It needs to be set for a specific task—'magazine promotion', or 'outreach'—and reviewed in the normal budgetary process of the church.

Advertising income

Although this might at first seem like a good way of getting a free, or low-cost, publication, there are both benefits and pitfalls for a magazine run either in part or in total by advertising income.

The benefits can include:

◆ considerably increased income

◆ a closer relationship with local business

◆ increased readership

◆ a service to the community.

But the pitfalls can include:

◆ a great deal of extra work that could be spent on other things

◆ a dilution of the communication aim of the magazine

◆ a conflict between editorial and advertising space

◆ potential difficulties when specific advertisements are declined because of ethical or religious principles

◆ in extreme cases, the risk of litigation when advertisements don't appear, appear wrongly, or are removed arbitrarily.

Sponsorship

Again, sponsorship might seem a good way of gaining extra income, and there are three forms of sponsorship:

◆ hidden sponsorship, where an individual or a company provide funds because they identify with the aims of the magazine and do not want explicit promotion

◆ overt sponsorship, where an individual or a company provide funds in order to raise their own profile in the community

◆ sponsorship in kind, where for example, a local company provides printing facilities free of charge in exchange for its name being credited on the cover.

Sponsorship is useful, provided that it is not relied upon from year to year, is identified in the budget, and the readers do not perceive the magazine as 'belonging' to the sponsoring organization. Sponsorship, even more than advertising, can change the perception of the magazine's values: it might no longer be perceived as an 'independent' publication.

Where funds are very tight, and a small church wants to promote a small outreach paper, it is possible to raise funds by asking supportive church members to subscribe to a sponsorship package. One possible package (though there are many different ways of doing this) is to ask supportive members to give £1 a week for this particular aspect of the church's outreach. If ten people are prepared to do this, a subsidy of £520 a year can be raised: quite enough to produce two or possibly three outreach newsletters a year.

Using syndicated inserts and material

There are a range of syndicated productions, from specific inserts stapled 'whole' into the centre of the magazine (*The Sign*, published in the UK, is one example) to articles, clip art and line drawings published monthly or bi-monthly for individual incorporation (Church News Service, published in the UK, is another example). The use of the former can give variety, and biblical teaching, to a low budget magazine of, say, two A4 pages folded to A5. The use of the latter can increase the range and variety of topics covered in a fuller magazine, and provide little fillers for those odd gaps.

Although syndicated material is often laid out in a way that allows it to be cut and pasted into a publication, the style and typeface used can contrast violently with the rest of the publication, and it is often a good idea (though admittedly time-consuming) to retype syndicated material, and edit it so that it conforms to the style of the rest of the magazine.

ADVERTISING

In nearly every newspaper, on all commercial radio stations, on independent commercial television, on buses and trains, at bus stops and on stations, in magazines and periodicals, there are bits of space and time that can be bought by individuals and companies so that they can communicate their particular messages. Within those spaces, for the period of time that has been bought, and subject only to the boundaries of perceived truth and the appropriate regulations, those individuals and companies can say whatever they like.

They can bring their product to the attention of a particular market; they can promote it against the competition; they can seek to change or influence opinion or behaviour; they can seek to change or influence people's perception of their organization; they can campaign or respond to campaigns; and they can disseminate information.

All this they can do because they have paid for that space and that time; they have hired, for a limited period and within defined boundaries, the medium of communication. The messages which operate in these defined spaces are called advertisements, and are defined as: 'Those messages which, because of the exchange of money or reciprocal favours, are originated by, and are under the control of, the advertiser.'

ADVANTAGES OF ADVERTISING

The advantages to the communicator of 'owning' a particular bit of space and time within which to communicate are enormous. Particular sections of the community can be fairly accurately targeted and reached; the messages will be placed at the time, and in the position, required; they will appear, and they will disappear, exactly as required; the content of the messages can be tailored to achieve exactly the tone, style and result that is required; and the effect can be accurately measured against the communication aim.

DISADVANTAGES OF ADVERTISING

The disadvantages are that the market forces of supply and demand make advertising space extremely expensive. Whole media industries are resourced from the income from advertising. The creation of effective advertising is in itself a huge industry, and the creation of an advertisement, its pre-testing and measurement, is as costly as the space it is designed to occupy.

The public, too, are wary of advertising, and can be downright cynical about its effects. Despite this, they often remember the humorous or catchy adverts, and can actually prefer some television advertisements to the programmes that surround them!

MAKING THE DECISION TO ADVERTISE

Using advertising as part of your communication plan is often both a bold and a necessary step. Other forms of communication are increasingly being denied to the church, where getting coverage in newspapers or on radio and television is more and more difficult. There are all sorts of factors that go into the decision-making process:

◆ Can the advertising achieve what is required of it?

◆ Can the messages be given in other ways?

◆ Does the benefit justify the cost?

◆ Is the campaign realistic in its aims?

◆ Will it alienate those it does not attract?

◆ Is it integrated with the rest of the campaign?

If the budget allows, it is probably best at least to consult an advertising agency. These companies will, if required, design, test and execute a campaign targeted against a particular group of people to achieve a particular aim from a brief provided by the client. Their services do not come cheap, and for most churches advertising will still be something that is self-originated.

This doesn't mean that the church shouldn't take the same care in defining the advertising campaign as an agency would, and many of the skills can be found within the congregations of many of our churches:

◆ A brief should be designed which sets out the people to be reached and the result required. (Note: it should not discuss message or execution at this stage.)

◆ From the brief, several different executions are worked up and suggested. These include the media options, a suggested message, and any visuals/sound effects.

◆ The client discusses the options and chooses one.

◆ The chosen option is brought to completion and tested against (a) the selected audience and (b) members of the client group. This is important, because although the advertisement needs to work with the target group, it should not alienate the clients!

◆ The campaign is run, and the results tested.

The creative, organizational and marketing skills needed to create an effective local campaign can often be found within the Christian community. If people with appropriate skills are not available in one congregation, then they can often be found in nearby churches.

THE DIFFERENT ADVERTISING MEDIA

There are a range of different advertising media available to the church, and each reach different groups of people and operate in different ways:

◆ newspaper advertising

◆ commercial radio advertising

◆ poster advertising

◆ television advertising

◆ cinema advertising

NEWSPAPER ADVERTISING

A newspaper advertisement can be as small as a classified ad, can increase in size through a display ad, or be as large as a half- or full-page ad. The advantage of newspaper advertising is that, being located in a word-based medium, it can convey complex arguments. People can put a newspaper down and pick it up again later, and the advertisement is likely to be read and re-read several times.

Newspaper advertisements, in local or regional newspapers, are affordable, at least by the larger congregations, or by churches working together.

It is also relatively easy to define the reach of a newspaper, and the advertising department can give penetration and circulation figures. Simply by reading it, the potential advertiser can come to some conclusions about the people he or she is likely to reach by advertising in it.

RADIO ADVERTISING

Advertising on commercial radio can be a highly effective way of reaching particular groups of people. It is more of a transitory medium, but a radio package will contain a number of 'plays' of the advertisement. The radio sales team will give you a breakdown of the number of 'opportunities to hear' based on the number of people listening at any one particular time.

Radio advertising can sustain an argument, though not as complex as one sustained by a newspaper advertisement. Listening to radio is both a primary and a secondary activity, and unless the advertisement is carefully put together, and has a good balance between words and sound effects, it is likely either to be missed, or to create an adverse reaction. There are specific rules in the UK and in many other countries with regard to religious advertising.

Many people balk at advertising on commercial radio because they don't think it is necessary to advertise their event across a whole region. But advertising on radio doesn't quite work like that. We tend to filter what we hear, and pay attention to the things that we recognize. We are unlikely to respond to an event advertised in a town at the other end of the county, but will pick up and respond to an event advertised to take place in our own or a neighbouring town.

Advertising on independent local radio can also be comparatively cost-effective. Many packages are often available for considerably less than their newspaper equivalents, and reach a much larger audience.

The creation of an advertisement for independent local radio is possible either through one of the specialist agencies, by the radio station itself, or through an advertising agency. As a charity, the church can sometimes get reductions in the creation cost, and particularly in the recurring royalties charged by voice-over artists.

A radio advertisement can be linked to a response mechanism such as the telephone enquiry line. See Chapter 22 for further details.

POSTER ADVERTISING

There is a difference between publicity posters created for space in shop windows, church notice-boards and supporters' gardens, and a full-scale poster advertising campaign on space bought from poster site owners. The difference is in cost and reach.

It might be more cost-effective to place a large poster on the side of a few buses than to print hundreds for distribution to church members: the reach will be that much greater, and the impact will equally increase.

Poster campaigns are created in the same way as any other campaign, but the way they operate is different. Although they are excellent attention-grabbers, they can only sustain a limited number of words, which makes any form of reasoned argument impossible. They can best be used to make a statement, or to challenge behaviour. The words need to be bold enough to be seen and taken in at one glance, and the visual needs to be distinct, but not over-complex. Poster campaigns can be linked to a response mechanism like the telephone enquiry line.

The cost of a commercial poster campaign is considerable, but it is possible to run a campaign on a limited budget by shopping around for creation, printing and poster space. Many site owners have unused space from time to time, and if your campaign is not time-critical, you might be able to benefit from this.

TELEVISION ADVERTISING

Advertising on regional and national television is unlikely to be within the financial means of any single church, and probably outside the means of most groups of churches. Even if the finance is available, television campaigns should not be run without at least discussion with the national office of the denomination concerned, and probably not without their specific approval.

This is because even regional television covers a very large area, and can create potent messages which may clash with, or even contradict, the carefully designed communication plan of a national church body. With the advent of the 1990 Broadcasting Act, churches in the UK are likely to suffer more and more from the uncoordinated enthusiasms of individuals and para-church organizations, and whilst their energy and motivation are kingdom-based, there is the real risk of damaging what other sections of the Christian church is doing.

With this word of caution, television advertising holds the promise of considerable advantage for the communication of the church's message. The author does not agree with those who, in the current debate, claim that television advertising will undermine the credibility of the church, or that it will associate it too closely with consumer goods. Our theology tells us that there is nothing created that is not redeemable. The experience of Christian charities who have used television advertising shows that, with careful creation and pre-testing, a television advertising campaign can have a real impact in changing the awareness, perception and education of the viewer.

The church has always adopted the best methods of communication available to it. For the church to ignore advertising and television today would be like St Paul ignoring the boat, or Luther ignoring the printing press.

CINEMA ADVERTISING

This is one area of advertising that holds real promise for the Christian churches, yet one that has hardly been used. Cinema audiences are increasing, and with the growth of multi-screen leisure centres, and ever-increasing audiences of all ages, the local church has much to gain from commissioning and making advertisements to be screened at the local cinemas.

The creation of a cinema advertisement is not something that can really be undertaken by an amateur with a film camera. If a group of local churches consider this an option in their communications plan, they should approach a local advertising agency for advice, or find someone who works in the world of advertising who can give them some helpful advice.

better to spend time getting the campaign right, than rushing ahead into something that neither you nor your local church can fully own and be proud of.

STAYING IN CONTROL

A final word on advertising and the church: it is easy to get steam-rollered by a combination of enthusiasm and professional advice. Don't be rushed into a campaign with which you are unhappy. If an agency makes a presentation that you don't like, don't be afraid of rejecting it. It is far

22 FREEPOST, RESPONSE MECHANISMS AND DIRECT MAIL

Most communication requires a response. That response can come in a whole variety of ways, from attendance at meetings or services of worship to a change of attitude or awareness. Using some form of response mechanism helps to provide a channel for enquirers to use, but also gives out a strong message that the enquirer's response is actually welcome.

There are three main forms of response mechanism open to most churches, and it's surprising that they are not used more often:

◆ the business reply envelope

◆ the freepost address

◆ the telephone answering machine.

BUSINESS REPLY

This is a form of prepaid envelope or response coupon which allows a respondent to write to you, or return a coupon to you, post free. There are several advantages:

◆ It's easy to use, allowing people to act on the first impulse, without having to find a stamp or an envelope, or spend time going to the post office.

◆ By using it, you are underlining the fact that you are prepared to pay for their reply, thus giving a strong message that their reply is wanted.

◆ It acts as an incentive to the originator, who has to focus his or her mind on designing the literature to gain the required response.

◆ Business reply envelopes or response coupons are pre-printed with the correct address, so there's less chance of the mail going astray.

One diocese had difficulty getting its busy clergy to reply to requests for routine administrative information. The next time they sent out the request, they enclosed a business reply envelope. The result was that nearly all the clergy responded within a week of the mailing!

Setting up a business reply system is relatively easy. There is an annual licence fee, and a certain number of replies have to be pre-paid in advance. There is a small surcharge (around 2.7 per cent) on the postage for each reply, but this is a small price to pay given that every response represents someone who really does want whatever it is that is on offer.

Business reply can be used both in letter form, and as the address on the reverse of a response coupon (although the coupon would have to be made from some form of card to comply with the postal authority's requirements).

THE FREEPOST ADDRESS

This is a variation on the business reply envelope, and operates in much the same way. It is very useful for response coupons, because someone can write to you without a stamp, but also without having to cut the coupon out! As with the business reply, there is an annual licence fee to pay, a number of replies have to be paid in advance, and there is a small surcharge on the postage cost of the reply (again, around 2.7 per cent).

THE POST OFFICE BOX NUMBER

It can be helpful to combine a business reply or freepost address with a PO box number. The advantage of a box number is that all the mail relating to the particular campaign is kept together, and does not have to be sorted from the organization's regular mail. Everything with that particular PO box number relates to that campaign. Neat, tidy and efficient.

Again, there is a small licence fee to pay for a box number, but it is easily within the budget of any moderate communications plan. The licence fee can be reduced if you decide to collect your own box mail, rather than have it delivered.

There is one disadvantage in using a PO box, however. Quite properly, some people are very suspicious about religious organizations that don't give their address. We have seen too many cults and weird religious groups operating to take anything at face value. A campaign offering free Christian literature run by the most established and respectable church in the community is likely to be looked on rather suspiciously by the person reading the following address:

Enquiry Office
Freepost,
PO Box 190
Anytown AN1 2TO

With a rise in proper and correct concern in society over the activities of cults and other weird religious groups, it can pay to ensure that the address spells out who the letter is actually going to, and therefore who will be behind the response:

The Vicar,
St. Mark's Church,
Freepost,
PO Box 190
Anytown AN1 2TO

Now that address must be absolutely above suspicion, mustn't it? In case even that causes suspicion, the Post Office will always disclose the name and address of the owner of the PO box. But not many people know that, and even if they did, few are going to take the trouble to find out before they throw the coupon in the bin! So before rushing headlong into getting a PO box, put yourself in the position of the enquirer, and ask whether you would have absolute confidence in the address.

THE TELEPHONE ANSWERING MACHINE

The telephone is a superb response mechanism. Eighty-eight per cent of British people have a telephone in the house, and there are telephone boxes within walking distance in most towns. It doesn't cost a lot to rent an 'incoming calls only' telephone line (which safeguards you from running up enormous bills because someone 'just thought their aunt in Australia was in need of fellowship'), and when there is no one there to answer it, it can be switched to an answering machine with a message tape.

The message tape can either be recorded to give a set of information (such as service times, the programme for a mission, etc.), or it can ask the caller for their name, address and telephone number so that you can get back to them or send them the appropriate literature.

The enquiry line/answering machine combination can be used in a number of communications plans, not least in poster and radio advertisements, where large amounts of information are not possible. The advertisements can both draw attention to the mission or festival and give the telephone number of an enquiry line, thus effectively combining targeted advertisement, response mechanism, and information base. If the church is really keen on this form of response mechanism, it is possible to get a freephone number in much the same way as the post office provide the freepost address. The distinctive freephone code is a real invitation for people to ring.

There is one major disadvantage to the freephone number. You will have to pay for all the calls that are made on that number, and unlike the business reply envelope (which you can limit) or the freepost address (where there is less novelty value) there is absolutely no control over the number of people who might telephone your freephone number.

DIRECT MAIL

Most of us are on someone's direct mailing list. If you've ever filled in a competition coupon, your name will have been entered on a direct mailing list. If you've responded to a clip coupon, again you will be put on a list. Every time someone sends you direct mail, they will have bought a list from a mailing house which happens to have your name and address on it.

These lists can be targeted very closely. If you want to write to all those families living in a specific geographical area who have two incomes, no children, a pet budgie and an expensive car, you can probably find a mailing house that will claim to be able to produce the list for you. But these lists are expensive.

Direct mailing for the church is one way of making contact with large numbers of people, and as most of us actually like receiving letters, the mailshot can be very effective in getting read. It can be combined with a business reply envelope, or a freepost reply address, and the surprise element of getting a direct mailshot from your local (or not so local) church will inevitably increase its effectiveness.

The difficulty of getting an address list can be overcome if the mailshot is related to a particular geographical area because the local authority electoral register can be used.

Mailing houses do not give their lists away, for obvious reasons, and do the stuffing and mailing of envelopes themselves, charging appropriately for the job. So unless the budget is reasonable, and direct mail is the central plank of the communication plan, it is probably not cost-effective for a small church to use a specialist list. However, the electoral register is cheaply and widely available, and can easily be used for specified geographical areas.

23 DISPLAYS, EXHIBITIONS, NOTICE-BOARDS

THE STATIC DISPLAY

Static displays are useful wherever people gather in reasonable numbers. They are used for awareness campaigns, and the ideal response is: 'Oooh, I didn't know they did that!'

An unattended static display might consist of two or three display boards with block-mounted photographs of church activities, worship and home groups, the minister at work in the community, or the youth leader taking young people on an expedition, together with some text explaining the activities, and a display box of pick-up leaflets. It might be used in various places around a town for a week at a time: the local leisure centre or swimming pool, the library, doctors' or dentists' waiting rooms, or the entrance hall of the local junior school.

It's important to keep a static display looking 'fresh', and any vandalized photographs should be replaced as soon as possible. Expect some vandalism to an unattended static display, prepare replacement material, and be delighted when you don't need it!

An attended display can be very useful, as long as those who are looking after it don't put people off by overenthusiasm. Preaching, or overt evangelism, usually creates an embarrassed space around the preacher, and if he or she is located by the display, all that will be achieved is to keep people away from it. It can help to have some activity taking place around the theme of the display. For example, if the theme is the young people's work of the church, it can help to have some of the young people there taking part in an activity (suitable for the environment). Leaflets or handbills are useful for continuing the contact, as are invitation cards to visitors' services.

THE TAPE–SLIDE DISPLAY

Tape–slide displays, and static videos are one step more technical than the straightforward display, but serve the same purpose. Tape–slide productions are reasonably cheap to make, and can be very effective. Their great advantage is that one or two slides can be changed (especially if personnel change) and the tape edited without having to remake the complete presentation. One of the really good things about tape–slide presentations as part of a static display is that people can watch them fairly anonymously. They don't feel 'preached at', and can pick up a leaflet about the church and its activities for further reference.

Tape–slide presentations can be very sophisticated, with cross-fades between two slide machines, and stereo sound effects. They can also be difficult to set up in a busy space! There's no need, however, to go to these lengths, or even to worry about slide projectors in a busy shopping mall. You can get some very good tape–slide display machines which simply present a screen with a picture and sound (rather like a small, square television set). These make an excellent adjunct to a static display. Tape–slide presentations can also be transferred to video tape fairly quickly and cheaply, making them an excellent medium for display purposes.

DESIGN, LAYOUT AND COST

Whether attended or not, static displays do need to be well-designed, look smart and be robust enough for the job—which means they are going to cost money. The basic structure can, of course, be used and re-used with only a change of material. But there is a considerable effort needed in designing a static display, as well as the money for the materials.

THE EXHIBITION

This is even more important when you are considering taking part in a major exhibition or county show. Your stand, as well as the display material, needs to be robust enough to last the course, and designed so that it doesn't look too shoddy against the five-thousand-pound 'one-off' design by Super Rich Computers Inc. Exhibition stands are expensive both in materials and time, and although it is possible to work off a table from the church hall covered with Mrs Jones' tablecloth, the messages that you will be giving may not necessarily be the ones you want to give.

For this reason, it's important to consider: 'Do I really want to be at this exhibition? What will be the benefits? What are the costs involved? Will the benefits justify the costs?'

NOTICE-BOARDS

As yourself what your notice-board is for. Is it:

◆ a label that identifies the building?

◆ an announcement about the kind of church you are?

◆ a source of information?

◆ a display for the times of the services?

◆ a badge that identifies your church's theology?

◆ aimed at Christians?

◆ aimed at those outside the Christian community?

◆ a place to stick posters?

Whatever you decide your notice-board is for, it should be part of the overall communications plan for your church. If there is a church 'logo', it should feature prominently on the notice-board. If there is a house 'style', using a set of colours, they should be reflected in the design of the notice-board.

Look at your existing notice-board (or get someone who doesn't go to church to look at it for you). What messages does it give? Is it in good repair? Does it 'fit' the existing style of the church?

A notice-board should attract people. It should be a 'hook' to draw their attention to the details it gives about the church and its activities. It should always have a contact telephone number, preferably the telephone number of the minister and the number of the church office if there is one, together with an address. It should give people the information they need: for example, will a couple wanting to arrange their wedding be able to find the minister's house by looking at the notice-board? Will someone wanting help or support in a crisis be able to find it?

Some churches have commissioned local artists to provide the visual 'hook' for their notice-board, to very great effect. An artistic interpretation of the symbol for St Mark, say, provides a very good visual, involves the local community, and states something important about the church.

THE SIGNPOST

Signposts are very useful to point the way to the church, and on a more discrete scale, they can be used inside the building. The local authority will be able to advise on both the placing and the wording of external sign-posts, and these can be very effective for new churches, or churches in very mobile urban areas.

Equally, discrete signs inside the church buildings can help people find their way around. A sign saying 'Entrance' not only points to the way in, but issues a quiet invitation. A sign saying 'Set apart for prayer' gives another form of invitation.

Churches that have a large number of tourists can benefit from a discreetly signed tour of the church, taking the tourist around the church in an ordered way, pointing not only to the architectural merits of the building, but to the theology and mission that shaped them.

COORDINATING YOUR MEDIA CHOICES 24

Designing and executing a communications plan is a mixture of science and art: there needs to be a careful process of data collection, analysis, design and execution, but within the design and execution there is need for artistry, colour, symbolism, mystery and surprise. We have so far looked at both of these aspects. The first section of this book dealt mainly with the careful 'putting together' of the communications plan: the data collection, preparation, design and execution. This second section has looked at the various textures and colours available through the various media available to the church communicator. The third section will look in greater depth at some of the theory that lies behind good communication.

First, in this chapter we will spend just a little time looking at how the various media choices can be put together. These are the colours and textures on your artist's palette, and they need to be mixed and put together in an imaginative and attractive way.

DEVELOPING A VISUAL STYLE

Whether you are designing a communications plan for a church, a mission, a festival or a party, it helps if every piece of literature, notepaper, compliments slip, and notice-board has the same feel to it. The logo, typeface, colours and general 'feel' need to be carried right through the plan. It's a way of saying, 'This belongs to the mission,' or, 'This is part of Anytown Baptist Church.'

There are several hints that can help you get this consistency of 'feel' throughout the plan:

◆ Always try to keep the logo in the same place, and in the same proportion. If it's on the top left of the notice-board, then try to keep it on the top left of the notepaper and compliments slips.

◆ Use the same typeface for notice-board, letter headings, printed material and tickets.

◆ Use colour subtly, to maintain continuity, or to emphasize change. The background colour to the notice-board might be the same as the notepaper or the brochure. A subtle change in base colour might indicate a sub-family of materials: details of seeker services, events or contacts might be highlighted by a change in background colour.

◆ Always use the same titles and headings for notepapers and brochures, and don't be afraid of quoting from the mission statement as part of the heading. This can help both to create identity and purpose.

For example: 'St Mark's United Church, Anytown' is a reasonable statement of identity, but adding a phrase from the mission statement helps. Here are a couple of possibilities:

St. Mark's United Church, Anytown
CELEBRATING LIFE TOGETHER

Anytown Council of Churches
WORKING FOR UNITY

Taking the idea a stage further, it can sometimes be helpful to design a short statement which describes the event, the festival or the church, and which can be added in small print to literature and brochure. This is particularly helpful where the event or church is not easily and directly understood. For example, putting the following tag on the noticeboard, notepaper and literature of 'Anytown Christian Centre' might help:

Anytown Christian Centre is supported by Baptist, Church of England, Methodist and United Reformed Churches working together.

The statement is one of image and identity, but helps people who are not regular church members to feel 'safe'. After all, 'Anytown Christian Centre' on its own might just be some weird kind of faith-healing centre, or even a cult group! But who can possibly be worried about the Church of England or the Baptists?

DEVELOPING A STYLE SHEET

If necessary, develop a 'style sheet', which is a printed document setting out the typeface, colours, logo artwork, and any basic rules about their use and who can use them. It can also include an outline of the communications plan for the church. This 'style sheet' can be given to all the organizations of the church so that they can work in harmony with the communications plan.

Think creatively, and don't be afraid of trying new ideas or of discarding old ones. The first person to think of presenting a gift to a charity by way of a huge cardboard cheque gained a great picture story, and no doubt a similar amount of publicity. But now that banks have stocks of large cardboard cheques ready for any charitable gift that their customers care to make, they are almost hackneyed. So try, where possible, to come up with fresh ideas. Don't be afraid of borrowing from other churches or organizations, or of adapting an idea that has worked well elsewhere.

SOME EXAMPLES

A COMMUNICATIONS PLAN FOR A CHURCH PLANT

The communication aim is to develop awareness of a proposed church plant on a new estate. The church wants to grow slowly, first of all inviting Christians from existing churches living in the area (with the full support of the church leaders) to consider supporting the new church. Then, once the core group is established, there will be a second phase of evangelism in the new area. The new church will meet initially in a house on the estate, moving to a community centre when the time is right. The church leaders want you to prepare a communications plan to help achieve the first stage.

Clearly, the process is initially an internal one. The first task is to draw together a core group of Christians from existing churches in the area to support the new church plant. There are two clear target groups:

◆ Christians from all churches living in the area of the proposed church plant who might join it

◆ other church members, who will need to know what is happening, and will need to feel secure in supporting their friends who might make the move.

However, there is some discussion about whether or not to include a third target group: the residents of the new church's area. Some argue that the church is not established and it is assumed that it is not yet ready to receive newcomers. Others argue that there would be concern in the community if it was felt that they were being 'got at' without knowing what was happening. You are concerned that local media should be encouraged to respond positively to the idea.

The issue is referred to the church leaders, who ask your advice. You offer them the following:

◆ Estate residents are added to the first stage communications plan so that the vision for a new church on their estate is shared with them, and their reactions and suggestions are sought.

The suggestion is accepted, and the budget is fixed. Having researched the extent of the denominational involvement, the number of existing churches and their membership lists, and the number of houses in the new church's area, you propose the following communications plan:

◆ A brochure should be prepared which sets out the vision for the new church. It is aimed primarily at the existing church membership, but will be jargon-free so that it can be used with residents.

The brochure will put forward a vision which shows that there is plenty of room for those taking part to shape the church to their needs. It will have a response form with a freepost address, which will help to establish a list of people wanting to be kept informed about the new church and ask if there are any specific needs that the new church should focus on (for example, children's work, youth work, mothers and toddlers groups, etc.). The brochure is delivered to all residents and small businesses in the geographical area of the proposed new church.

SECTION TWO: MEDIA OPTIONS

- ◆ A letter should be designed for members of all the existing churches explaining the new venture, asking for their prayers and support, and seeking to establish potential new members of the church. It too will have a response form with the same freepost address so that those people interested in joining the new church can register their interest, and seek a discussion with the new church leader when he or she is known.

- ◆ A media briefing should be held so that the process of establishing a new church can be explained, together with the aim of growing slowly and building on existing members. The vision brochure will be available.

- ◆ A news release is designed to compliment the media briefing, and a question-and-answer sheet is prepared.

- ◆ Three editions of a new four-page leaflet (A3 folded to A4) should be planned over the following twelve to eighteen months aimed at residents of the new church's area, which will keep them up to date with progress towards the establishment of the new church. These leaflets will be sent to local media outlets when they are distributed.

- ◆ A press and communication person should be appointed from amongst the emerging members of the new church to take on the running of the communications plan in due course. The task will include working with the new members to develop the identity of the church within the community, and to raise awareness of its growth and development by appropriate media and communications.

A LOCAL MISSION RUN BY A GROUP OF CHURCHES

You have been asked to develop a 'publicity' plan for a mission to be held in nine months' time. Organized by a group of churches in the area, it will take the form of a 'Festival of Christian faith', and will seek to involve as many of the social, political and community organizations as possible in thinking about the values that are important for the community.

There are several initial tasks which you propose to the steering committee:

- ◆ the formation of a communications team
- ◆ the establishment of an outline budget
- ◆ the designation of a 'link person' in each participating church.

At the first meeting of the team you develop your communication aims. These are:

To bring together the ideas and proposals from the various churches in a way that enables the Christian community to be fully aware of every aspect of the mission.

To gain full awareness and participation within the local community.

The initial internal communication consists of the following:

- ◆ A team of 'link people' is developed, by inviting the appropriate person from each church to a regular meeting to share ideas and to develop the programme in an integrated way.

- ◆ An identity is created for the festival, consisting of a logo, a tag line description and a style sheet, together with artwork for churches to use.

◆ A tape–slide presentation is put together for the various churches which presents the identity of the festival. Each participating church is featured, together with a description of the events and activities they will be offering to the festival, and shows people how they can get involved.

The tape–slide presentation is given to all the organizations of each church by the link person, followed by discussion.

The external communication of the festival consists of the following:

◆ an information office with a direct information line with a distinctive telephone number, attended during office hours and on an answering machine outside office hours

◆ an advertising programme using forty-eight-sheet and four-sheet posters with an appropriate visual, using the logo and giving the information line number, and a series of radio advertisements aimed at families and young people, again giving the information line number

◆ a single A2 full-colour poster, folded into A5 size, giving a map of the town with the locations of the churches, pictures of the church activities, contacts for the various churches, the information line number and a full programme for the festival for distribution to every household in the town

◆ a media briefing featuring two of the 'star attractions'—the key speaker and a leading Christian sportswoman

◆ a range of badges, balloons and beer mats for free distribution

◆ a car sticker distributed in exchange for a contribution to publicity funds.

In addition to the direct publicity plan, several of the churches decide to get together to run a special-event radio station during the festival. The aim of the station will be to reach every home in the festival area with entertainment, news, features and local personalities not only from the churches but from the many social, political, commercial and cultural groups in the area. The frequency of the station is carried on every item of publicity, and posters and handbills are created to raise awareness of the station's frequency.

A television company is told about the station, and decides to do a feature on it, thus adding to the publicity profile of the festival.

SECTION THREE

COMMUNICATION THEORY

25 UNDERSTANDING COMMUNICATION SYSTEMS

In the first part of this book we looked at the process of constructing a communications plan. In the second part, we looked at the various media options that could be used in its construction. Like a recipe book, the ingredients from the second part could be mixed together according to the eleven-step process so as to produce a communications plan that would fit the communication aims that had been defined.

But in this third and final section we go a little further, and look at some of the theory behind the process. Putting the theory last is quite deliberate, because in order to understand it we need to have had some practical experience on which to reflect. It is not necessary to understand the basic theory in order to construct a communications plan that works, but like any discipline, the more we can understand, the better practitioners we shall become.

First, we need to grasp four basic concepts. The names we give these concepts are in one sense completely arbitrary—they could be called anything. But in another sense, the names reflect something which is analogous to the concept itself:

- task
- role
- boundary
- system

TASK

People get together in order to engage in tasks. The task may be a complex one, like designing an aeroplane, or it may be a simple one, like creating music in a church choir. But whether complex or simple, the task is producing the 'end product' that is sought by the people who come together to achieve it.

ROLE

People take up roles in order to achieve tasks. A number of roles are needed in order to complete the task. With the construction of an aeroplane, there are a vast number of roles required to be exercised before the aeroplane takes shape and flies. With the creation of music in a church choir, the number of roles are limited. For example, a good church choir can be created with:

- four sopranos or trebles
- two contraltos or altos
- two tenors
- two basses
- one conductor
- one accompanist

Twelve roles in all, and each need filling by a person willing and qualified to take up that role.

BOUNDARY

Tasks are achieved within defined boundaries. At work, I might be an aircraft designer. On Thursday evenings and for part of Sunday I may be a tenor in the church choir. At other times I might take up many different roles: parent, student, teacher, aircraft designer, tenor, church elder, and so on. But each of these roles is exercised within geographical and chronological boundaries. The boundaries are important in that they define when it is appropriate to exercise a particular role, and when it is inappropriate.

The boundaries are also important in that they help me focus on the task that is to be achieved. From 7.30 p.m. until 9.30 p.m. on a Thursday evening in church, the task I am engaged in is creating choral music. From 9.00 a.m. until 5.00 p.m. on weekdays at the aircraft factory, the task I am engaged on is creating a new aircraft. At different times and in different places I am exercising different roles to achieve different tasks with different groups of people.

SYSTEM

A system is a group of people taking up roles within a defined boundary in order to complete a task. The church choir is a system; the aircraft factory is a system; the church of which I am an elder is a system; the family in which I am a parent is a system. In fact, most of us take up roles within a vast network of separate or interconnected systems.

SYSTEM REPRESENTATION

The system can be represented by a simple drawing. The large, encompassing circle represents the boundary. The smaller circles represent the roles that are necessary to achieve the task that the system is there to achieve. The task is written at the bottom of the drawing, and the roles are listed.

Let's see how a church choir is drawn when it is represented as a system:

SECTION THREE: COMMUNICATION THEORY

The Church Choir

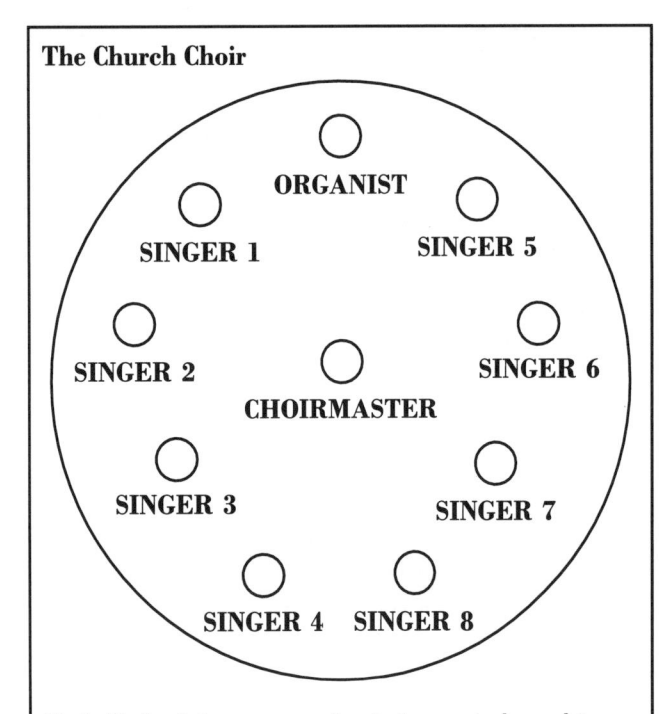

(Diagram: a circle with CHOIRMASTER at centre; around the circle are ORGANIST at top, SINGER 1 and SINGER 5 upper left/right, SINGER 2 and SINGER 6 middle left/right, SINGER 3 and SINGER 7 lower left/right, SINGER 4 and SINGER 8 at bottom.)

Task: To lead the congregation in its musical worship (Note: Not to perform, nor to act as an alternative youth club!)
Roles:
Singers 1 & 2   to sing treble
Singers 3 & 4   to sing alto
Singers 5 & 6   to sing tenor
Singers 7 & 8   to sing bass
Choirmaster   to lead the choir and direct the music
Organist   to prvide musical accompaniment

MULTIPLE OR COMPLEX SYSTEMS

The church choir is a simple system. It has clear boundaries, and provided that the numbers are kept fairly small, it can operate as a single system on a single task. But not all systems are as simple as the church choir. For example, very few church choirs exist on their own. They are usually part of a larger system called a church. That the church is a system is clear because it has a task ('to provide a community for disciples' might be one task definition), it has boundaries (you are a member of the church, or you are not), and roles are required to enable it to achieve its task (minister, member, elder, etc.). But within the system we know as 'church', there may be any number of smaller systems operating to assist the task.

For example, the following smaller systems may be operating within the larger system of the church:

◆ elders' meeting
◆ church meeting
◆ church choir
◆ house group
◆ women's fellowship
◆ youth group
◆ social committee

Each of these is a complete system in itself, because each has a clearly discernible task, each require definable roles to achieve that task, and each takes place within specific boundaries. What is more, one person can take up a different role in each of these systems. I am a tenor in the church choir. I am an elder in the elder's meeting. I am a member in a house group. Three distinct roles within three separate systems taken up by the same person.

These smaller systems need to relate to each other if the church is to operate as a healthy system. And the way they relate to each other is by using the process of internal communication. Let's look at how these different systems can be represented in diagrammatic form. From now on, where the system referred to is part of the larger system being described, we will use a small

Three smaller systems within a larger system

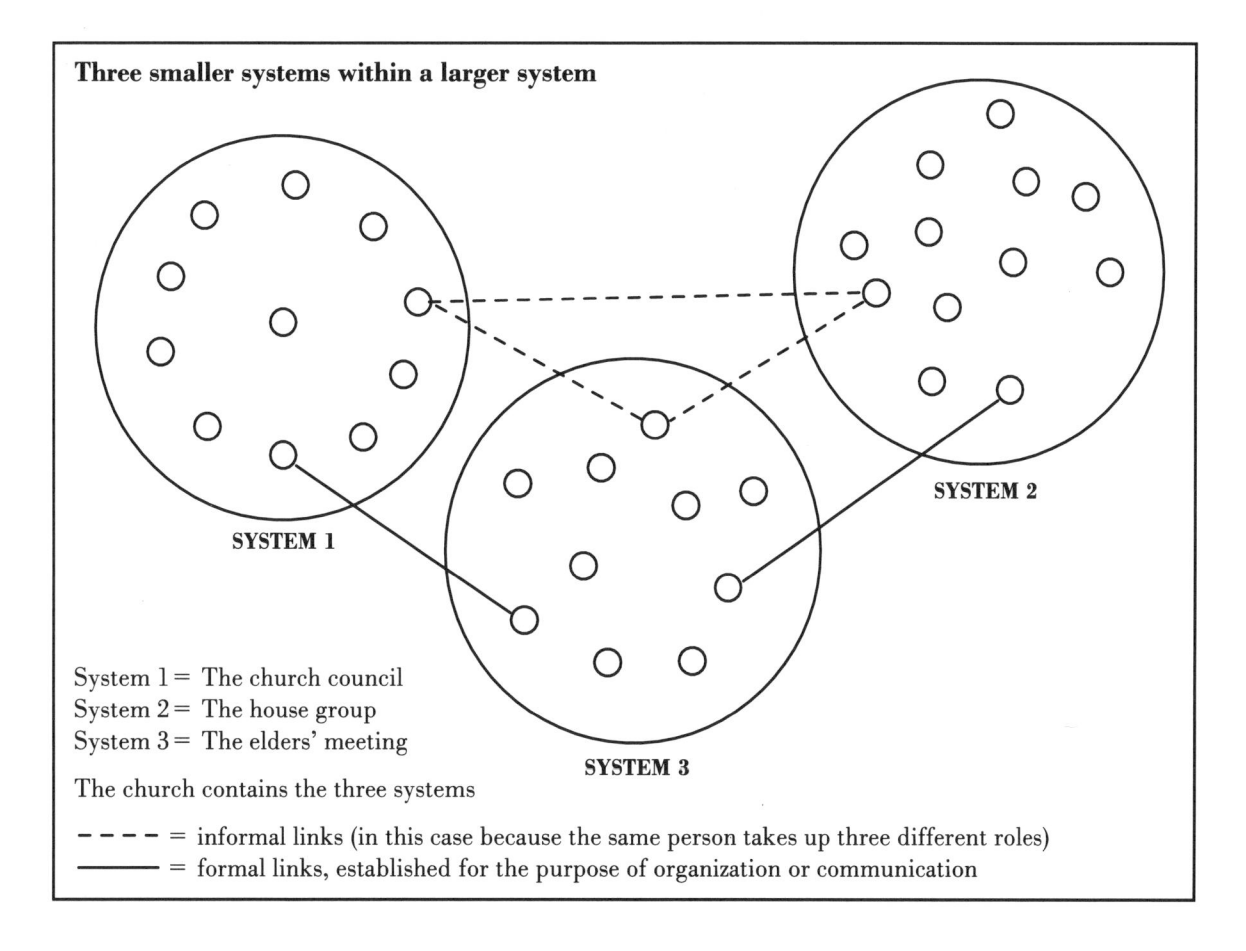

System 1 = The church council
System 2 = The house group
System 3 = The elders' meeting
The church contains the three systems

– – – – = informal links (in this case because the same person takes up three different roles)
───── = formal links, established for the purpose of organization or communication

's'. Where the system being described is made up of smaller, internal systems, we will use a capital 'S'.

Using our diagrammatic way of representing systems, their relationship might be drawn as follows:

SYSTEM DYSFUNCTIONS

Communication problems can happen both as a cause and a result of things going wrong with a system. Very often, the communication practitioner is called in to sort out a 'communication problem' which turns out to be a system dysfunction of some sort. There are three symptoms to look out for:

◆ conflict and aggression

◆ 'opting-out', flight, disintegration

◆ stuckness, or inability to achieve the task.

Any one of these symptoms might point to any one of a number of difficulties within, or between systems. But there are five basic dysfunctions that we need to be aware of, and which can be presented to us as 'communications' problems:

- task confusion
- role confusion
- boundary slip
- skill conflict
- isolation.

Task confusion

Task confusion occurs when one or more members of any particular system hold different understandings of the task of the system. Here's a particular example, based on the simple system of the church choir.

The choirmaster has set high standards for his choir. He is careful to rehearse any piece for at least four weeks before it is used in worship. He trains the children separately before the adults arrive for a joint rehearsal each week, and uses a nationally recognized points system for their achievement.

However, the choir is becoming increasingly annoyed at the new minister, who has on three occasions brought young children at the start of choir practice, expecting the choirmaster to accept them into the choir straight away. The minister has expressed considerable surprise, and private annoyance, that these children have not been immediately welcomed and taken into the choir.

This is a classic case of task confusion between the minister and the choir. There are two potential tasks in conflict:

- to produce music to the highest possible standard
- to provide an alternative 'youth group' to bring children into church.

If the minister had his way, the task of producing good music would give way to a more important task of bringing children into church. If the choirmaster had his way, the production of music to the highest standard would mean that some children would not be suitable for the choir!

A great deal of energy can be diverted into this conflict, with both minister and choir increasingly distancing themselves from each other. Any of the following three symptoms can present themselves:

- conflict and aggression between the minister and the choir
- 'opting out', when the choirmaster, choir members or minster leave (the 'leaving' can be either a physical departure, or avoidance of the conflict by failing to resolve it)
- stuckness, when the choir increasingly fail to produce music to a high quality, or children continually fail to be integrated into the life of the church.

A discussion on the question 'What are we here to do?' can often elicit hidden conflicts over the task, and can be the way to restore health to the system by negotiating an agreed task. Here's how the conflict was resolved:

The choirmaster decides to hold a discussion with the minister. He starts by suggesting that they both write down what they think the choir is 'there to do'. Each produce a list. The minister's list is as follows:

- to lead the music in worship
- to use members' musical skills.

The choirmaster's list is as follows:

- to produce music for worship to the highest possible standard
- to train children and adults to sing
- to provide a social group within the church.

Hidden tasks

The lists are essentially the same, and there doesn't appear to be any task conflict at first. But this apparent 'same-ness' highlights one aspect of task confusion that often confuses even the most experienced communicator. It is this:

> **The task being achieved may differ considerably from the stated task!**

Or in this case, the task that the minister has listed as primary is not actually the primary task that he wants the choir to achieve. Whatever he might state, he is actually thinking, 'The church is there to provide a home for all sorts of people, and the choir is the best place for these new children because their friends sing in the choir, and they are more likely to stay in church if they're with their friends.'

So whatever he may be saying about good music, or members' skills, his actual primary task for the choir will read:

- to be one of the places where new children can be integrated into the life of the church

The choirmaster and the minister discuss their lists. Before long, the choirmaster asks the minister why, if he says he believes the first task of the choir is to produce good music, does he get annoyed when the choirmaster turns away children who can't sing a note in tune? The minister replies that it is more important to keep the children in church than to insist on their being able to sing professionally. At last, the conflict is on the way to being resolved because the choirmaster has skilfully elicited the task confusion!

Another example of hidden task confusion is often experienced over the task of the church itself. A mission statement which declares that the church is there:

- to reach out into the community with the love of Christ, and to train new Christians in discipleship (stated task)

can be contradicted by the hidden task being undertaken by the members, who behave as though:

- the church is there to provide fellowship, worship and teaching at times most convenient for us (actual task)

The hidden task confusion can be readily identified when a member suggests changing the service to a time when more members of a local housing estate are likely to be able to attend!

This difference between stated and apparent, or 'hidden', task may not be recognized consciously by the members of the system, and the people who take up roles within a system in order to achieve a stated task may well collude with a completely different, but 'hidden', task without realizing it until conflict occurs.

Task confusion can be a great barrier to good internal and external communication, and can provide fertile ground for conflict over a carefully prepared communications plan based on a stated task when the actual, but hidden, task is something different.

Role confusion

Role confusion occurs when a person behaves as though he or she is operating a different role from the one required by the system. Once again, we will use the example of the church choir to examine role confusion:

Mr Jones is the choirmaster. He is an amateur, self-taught musician who has led the choir for twenty-two years. He puts a great deal of energy into running the choir, and is delighted when Mr Smith, who is a music master at the local senior school, joins the choir to strengthen the tenor line.

But conflict soon begins to disrupt the choir practices. Mr Smith begins by making helpful suggestions, but is more and more behaving as though he were the choirmaster. Mr Jones feels unable to cope, and finally goes to the minister to resign.

This is a classic case of role confusion. Mr Smith has the role of 'choirmaster' in his school choir, and 'tenor' in the church choir. However, he is inappropriately importing his role as choirmaster into the system which requires him to be a tenor.

Role confusion can lead to considerable internal conflict within an individual, as well as external conflict between individuals. Feelings of frustration, impotence and rage can be generated when people take up roles that are different from the ones they thought they were taking up, or when they import role behaviour from the roles they exercise in other systems. Other people may collude with the inappropriate behaviour that is a symptom of role confusion, manipulating the feelings of frustration or rage for their own purposes. In our last example, Mr Smith might have been encouraged in his inappropriate role as 'choirmaster' by Mrs Bloggs, who wants to change the power structures within the choir.

Boundary slip

Boundary slip occurs when any of the boundaries get blurred, changed, become unclear, or begin to threaten the task. One symptom that indicates when boundary slip is occurring is a feeling of insecurity in the members of the group. The time boundaries get blurred when the meeting starts late, goes on too long, or people are unsure of when it should happen. The geographical boundaries change when the newsletter begins to be delivered in another church's territory, or when the group begins to lose touch with the amount of money being spent.

Boundaries are important because they keep the group focused clearly on the task, and it is usually part of the group leader's role to keep the boundaries intact. The group leader needs to ensure that all the members know when the group should begin to function; when the system is 'in place'. He or she needs to be clear about when the group should finish, and work to that time; where, geographically, the system functions, and where it ceases to function.

Boundaries are about helping people to feel that things are under control, and people not only like to feel that someone is in control: they need to know who it is and where that power is to be exercised. When the time boundaries are allowed to slip, people can feel that they are wasting time, or that things 'just aren't right'.

COMMUNICATION BETWEEN SYSTEMS 26

If each and every human activity were carried out within simple discrete systems, there would be no need for communication between them. The baker would bake his bread, and we would buy it. The musicians would play their music, and we would listen. The football team would challenge us at football, and we would win! But human life is not lived out in discrete systems. Musicians operate within orchestras, which form part of a production, which tours the country as part of a cultural display. Bakers set up shop within a supermarket, which is part of a national chain. Football teams join together in an association, which is represented on a sports council.

Within each complex System, there are often many smaller, discrete systems operating with their own tasks, roles and boundaries. Each has a relationship with the others in the same System, and with many others outside it. The way in which they relate is often a function of their health, and the task of constructing and maintaining good communication between and within Systems is part of the task of the communicator.

It helps to recognize that communication is a role that has to be taken up within a system. All systems need to communicate in some form: in fact, the word we use for any system that is not communicating is 'autistic', and autism is a seriously debilitating condition. The role of communicating within a system is either defined and owned by one of the members, or it is allowed to happen in a haphazard way. It can happen when one person takes up a role in each of two different systems, and becomes a bridge between them, or it can happen when one person from one system happens to meet with one person from another system and by chance they discuss issues or difficulties which relate to the relationship between the two systems.

You can see this happening (and indeed may well have been part of it yourself at some time) when two systems that have no formalized mechanism for communication come into conflict. Because of the pressure that is felt by each of the members to resolve the conflict, if any one of them comes into contact with any member of the other system, each acts like a lightning conductor, immediately responding to the systemic pressure to discuss, or even fight over, the conflict. But where the systems have formalized and defined a channel of communication between them, then the pressure that might otherwise have been felt by each of the members is relieved: the matter is being dealt with 'through the proper channels', and the members of the opposing systems can happily step out of their respective roles and chat happily together as common members in a third system.

SECTION THREE: COMMUNICATION THEORY

Let's try and demonstrate this by outlining a hypothetical conflict between two systems, and then representing it pictorially:

The choir has a great love of, and a great skill at performing, traditional baroque choral music. For them, a Bach chorale is an act of worship without parallel. There is a group within the church, however, which want congregational participation and lots of modern songs. This group has raised the issue at the church council, and there is to be a meeting of the council to discuss the matter. However, shortly before the meeting, one of the choir members (Mr Smith) 'has words' (strong words) with one of the PCC members (Mrs Jones) who was, until that point, a good friend.

What's happening to cause these two good friends to fall out? Let's try to represent the systems pictorially:

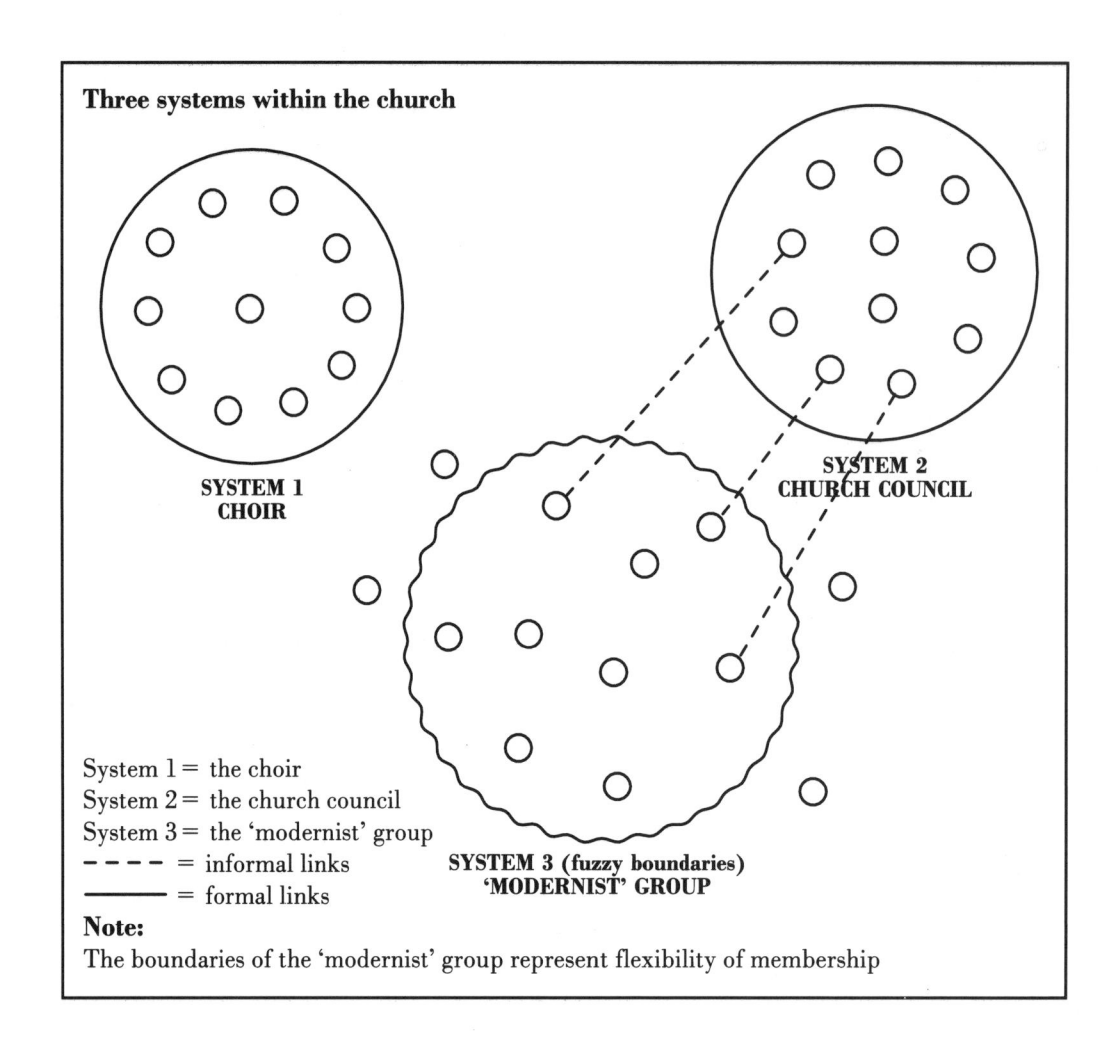

Three systems within the church

SYSTEM 1 — CHOIR

SYSTEM 2 — CHURCH COUNCIL

SYSTEM 3 (fuzzy boundaries) — 'MODERNIST' GROUP

System 1 = the choir
System 2 = the church council
System 3 = the 'modernist' group
- - - - = informal links
———— = formal links

Note:
The boundaries of the 'modernist' group represent flexibility of membership

Right away we can begin to see the difficulty. There is no formal channel of communication between the choir and the church council. Mrs Jones, who is a member of the council, used to be in the choir but has recently retired. She used to act as informal bridge between the two bodies because she took up roles in both. Furthermore, she has taken up a role as a member of the informal 'modernist' group.

It seems fairly clear that she is still behaving as though she were the informal link between the two bodies, but because of her membership of the 'modernist' group, none of the choir sees her as such.

The first lesson in communication between systems, or groups, is that it is dangerous to rely on informal links between groups. In a complex system, there need to be simple, structured channels of communication between the main system and its constituent sub-systems.

The way out of the dilemma outlined in the above example (as is so often the case), is to provide simple but formal channels of communication between the three groups, and to clarify their tasks. For example, the choirmaster could be appointed to the church council, the informal group is asked to put proposals to the church council and provide a member as representative, and the task of each of the groups is explored.

PRESENTING PROBLEMS

At the same time, it becomes clear that difficulties within systems can present themselves in all sorts of ways. Members may argue with each other, or may leave. They may express frustration, or may simply attempt to sabotage bits of work. Often feelings generated by system dysfunction are very strong, and the damage can take some time to heal.

PREVENTION IS BETTER THAN CURE

Communication between systems within a larger System, and between Systems themselves, is best managed by defining it as a task in its own right, and allocating that task to one of the roles within each system. If, for example, the choirmaster is allocated the task of communicating issues between the choir and the church council, it is essential that he attends the council meetings, and it can help if he takes up a role as a member of the council. Provided he acts as communicator within his own system (the choir), he will find that tensions between the two systems can be managed more effectively.

The isolation of one system within a larger System is always a recipe for conflict. It can help to draw a map of the various mini-systems operating within a larger System, drawing in the formal and informal links between them as solid and dotted lines. Those with plenty of solid lines will run well; those with only dotted lines, or no lines at all, are likely to run less well, and use up lots of energy in discussion of task or conflict.

SECTION THREE: COMMUNICATION THEORY

Diagram of System with isolated systems

SYSTEM 4
CLERGY STAFF

SYSTEM 2
HOUSE GROUP

SYSTEM 6
YOUTH CLUB

SYSTEM 5
WOMENS' GROUP

SYSTEM 3
CHURCH COUNCIL

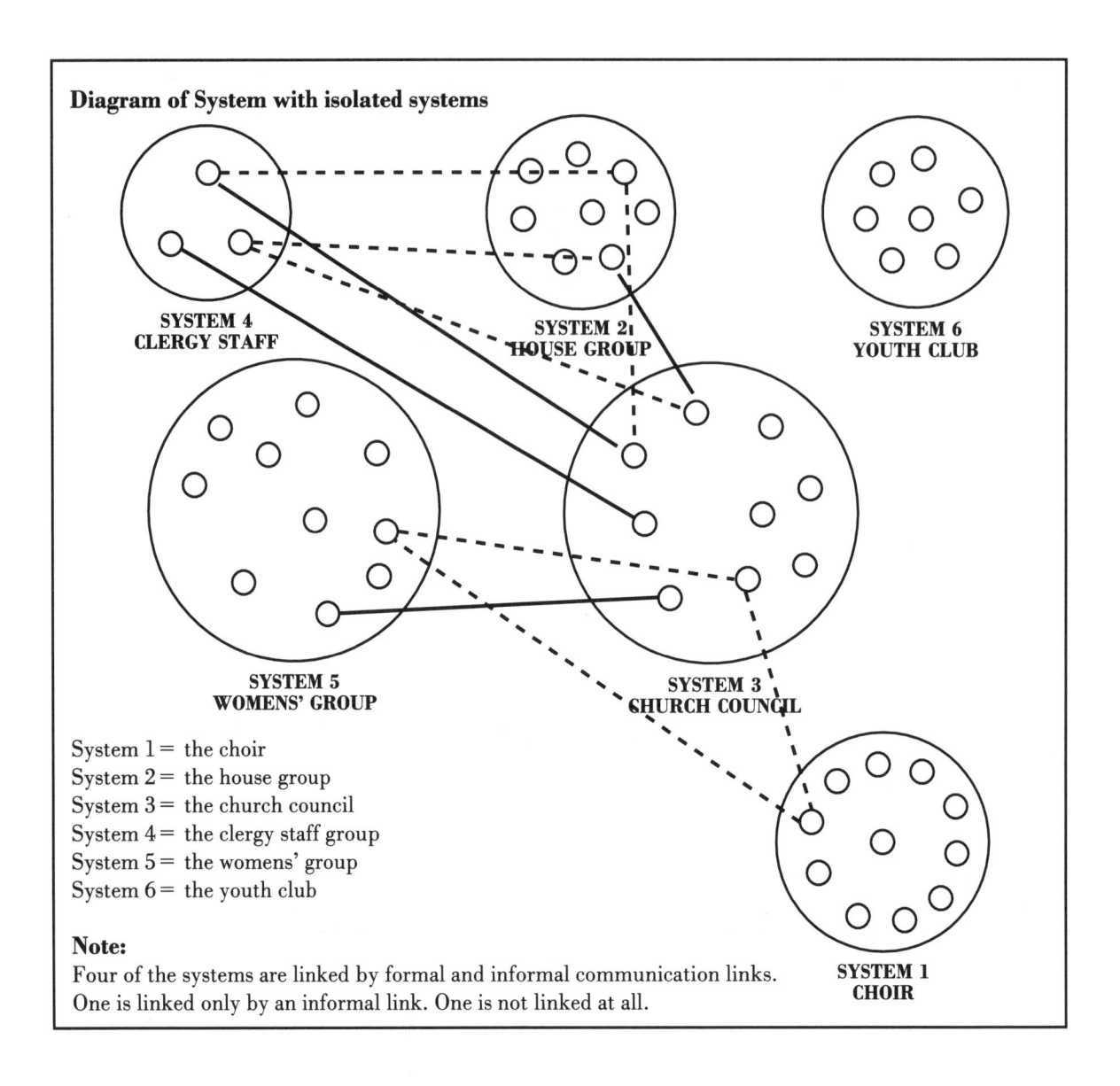

SYSTEM 1
CHOIR

System 1 = the choir
System 2 = the house group
System 3 = the church council
System 4 = the clergy staff group
System 5 = the womens' group
System 6 = the youth club

Note:
Four of the systems are linked by formal and informal communication links. One is linked only by an informal link. One is not linked at all.

Occasionally, communication between systems needs be managed on a grand scale. One example is the formal arbitration process; another is the annual conference. In the first case, it is the task of a third party to bring together representative people to meet across a table. In the second, it is the task of a third party to arrange a meeting together of all members of each system within commonly agreed boundaries. Either way, the aim is to encourage meeting and discussion in order to gain a common understanding and to facilitate the exchange of information, feelings and difficulties.

SYSTEMS WITHOUT TASKS

As well as task confusion, some systems fail to work because there is no task for them to engage in. This can happen for one of two reasons:

◆ It can happen because the original task has been achieved, but the members of the system, having enjoyed the sense of companionship and achievement gained by working on the task, have continued to meet. They might well search around for another task (which immediately identifies the hidden task as 'providing a place for this group of people to continue to feel they belong') which they happily and more or less constructively engage in, or they might simply feel increasingly frustrated and at odds with each other.

◆ It can also happen because someone suggests that a group be formed, but gives them an inappropriate, impossible or non-existent task. The group will continue to meet, but will spend a great deal of energy trying to define what it is there to do. It may discover a task, or it may invent one, or it may fade away, with members increasingly failing to turn up.

Whatever reason, a group without a task can present symptoms of distress in all sorts of ways within a church structure. Individuals can misdiagnose the problem as 'losing my faith', or 'the church losing its way', and it can result in quite dramatic exits by individuals. One of the roles taken up by the leader needs to be the monitoring of each system within the church to ensure that it is working to an agreed task. This task might be 'praying together', or 'supporting each other', but it does need to be agreed and it does need to be in operation. A group without a task is a disaster waiting to happen.

GETTING THE SYSTEM WORKING

As with the design of a communications plan, there are several clear steps we can take to ensure that a system is working well.

◆ Define the task clearly, agree it and make sure that it is appropriate and achievable.

◆ List the roles needed to ensure that the task can be achieved.

◆ Decide what skills are needed by the individuals who will take up those roles.

◆ Carefully define the boundaries.

Consider the following example:

Jim Smith was newly appointed as pastor of the local Baptist church. One of the first things that he discovered was that there was considerable discontent within a group that had been meeting to redesign the interior of the church. This discontent presented itself in two ways. First, two of the members of the design group had an argument at the deacons' meeting about whether the church really needed a new interior. Secondly, another member came to see him to say that she really felt that she was wasting her time as a member of that group.

Jim decided to have a systematic review of the group. He defined its task as:

To present to the deacons' meeting a range of options for re-designing the interior of the church by consulting with church members.

He then looked at the roles needed, and defined these as:

◆ *group leader*

◆ *three people to consult church members*

◆ *a secretary who would prepare a report.*

The skills and resources he identified for the roles were:

◆ *time to give to the project*

◆ *good consultative skills*

◆ *freedom from any 'special interest' group*

◆ *secretarial skills that included report writing.*

The boundaries Jim identified for the group were these:

◆ *the project should take no longer than three months*

◆ *it should not attempt to define a solution*

◆ *it should consult all groups within the church*

◆ *it should keep within a small agreed budget*

◆ *any sketch plans should be in outline only.*

He then called a meeting of the group to discuss the task, roles and boundaries. Not surprisingly, he found that there had been considerable disagreement about the task, mainly because the members had originally been selected to represent different groups from within the church, and had spent much time trying to convince the group of their own arguments so that it would present a favourable report to the deacons. Not only that, but the group had undertaken little consultation with members, and had virtually no data on which to reflect.

WORKING WITH TEAMS 27

Building and maintaining a communication team is a necessary part of any major communication project. Having spent some time looking at systems, how they work, and what can go wrong with them, it should now be possible to look at team building in the same light. In fact, the process of building and maintaining the team is an essential part of the success of most communications plans, and needs careful and constant work.

DEFINING THE TASK

The first step in any team-building process is to define the task or tasks that the team is going to achieve. As we have seen, a clear, agreed task is essential for the health and good working of any system, and your communication team is going to be just that: a healthy, energized system that has a clear task, clear boundaries, and appropriately skilled people taking up defined and agreed roles.

The task of the communication team is going to be closely allied to the aim defined in the communications plan. For example, let's take a simple plan of using posters to communicate the launch of a new youth programme. The communication aim has been defined:

To inform young people aged between 14 and 16 of a new youth programme, and to invite them to take part.

There is a four-week time-scale, and the communication medium chosen is a large poster campaign in schools, colleges, youth clubs and other places where young people gather.

The next step is to outline the roles needed to achieve the task. These are:

◆ identifying the sites for display

◆ budget management

◆ campaign design and poster production

◆ actual posting of the posters

◆ awareness monitoring

◆ time-keeping

◆ internal and external communication.

Some of these roles can be achieved by a single person with the appropriate skills. Others are likely to require more than one person. For example, the actual posting of the posters requires that for maximum impact they should all go up on the same day, and that in turn suggests a small team of people working to that end.

The next step is to find individuals who will take up the roles already identified. The team leader is the communication director, and she has carefully listed the skills required under each of the roles. This is important because it would be easy to disable the team by asking someone to take on a role for which they don't have the necessary skills. Roles could be defined as follows:

Identifying the sites for display

Skills needed: knowledge of the target audience, access to potential sites, practical common sense. Maybe a young person (or possibly two, as young people often feel threatened on their own in an adult environment).

Budget management

Skills needed: experience of financial control, basic book-keeping.

Campaign design and poster production

Skills needed: knowledge of target audience, access to design skills, knowledge of print processes.

Actual posting of the posters

Skills needed: a little muscle, common sense, possibly diplomacy. If this role is to be carried out by a sub-team, then the person appointed needs team-management skills.

Awareness monitoring

Skills needed: knowledge of the process, availability to carry out the monitoring, data-handling experience.

Time-keeping

Skills needed: experience of planning and executing a project, firmness of character, diplomacy.

Internal and external communication

Skills needed: access to the various groups with which communication will be necessary.

In addition, each member of the team will need sufficient time available to attend team meetings and to carry out their roles.

The team leader decides to take on the role of communicator, and recruits a team of six, each with the appropriate skills. She has to look outside her own congregation to find someone with design skills, but is able to negotiate with a neighbouring church to 'borrow' the ideal person for the duration of the exercise. (This kind of cross-fertilization is always very productive, provided that all the basic human fears about 'poaching' from other churches can be allayed at the start.)

THE FIRST TEAM MEETING

The task of the team leader at the first team meeting is to begin to weld the individuals into a team. In order for this to happen, the following things need to be achieved:

Each member needs to be introduced and known

If any of the members are unknown to the others, it can help to go around the group asking all members to introduce themselves in turn, and share a little of their background. No one can feel comfortable until they know, and have come to terms with, the power and skill structures within the group. Each needs to know who the others are, what experience they have, and what power they are likely to exercise.

The task needs to be shared and agreed

The basic question 'What are we here for?' needs to be addressed and answered. It is no good assuming that each member knows why they have been invited to join the team.

After the introduction of members, the team leader can begin by making a statement like: 'Thank you for agreeing to be part of this team. Our task over the next six weeks is to inform young people between 14 and 16 of a new youth programme, and to invite them to take part. To do this, we have provisionally agreed on a poster campaign, and each of you has been invited to help in a particular way which we can discuss in a moment. Does everyone understand the task?'

Questions for clarification of the task can lead to common ownership, or (on rare occasions) to an individual's disagreement with the task surfacing. If this happens, the team leader will need either to work with the individual concerned to bring them on board, or decide to recruit someone else. The media choice also needs to be agreed at the outset. It is no good continuing to build a team for a poster campaign if the majority present feel that an advertising campaign on the local radio station would be better.

Each member needs to know their own role

Once the task has been agreed and owned, the team leader needs to go through each of the roles required, and invite individuals to take up those roles. For example:

'First, we're going to need someone to identify and make a list of all the places where we can put up the posters. This needs someone who can find out where young people gather, and where the possible poster sites are. Jim, I wondered if you could take on this bit of the job?'

Each member needs to know other members' roles

As the meeting progresses, each member discovers not only his or her own role but also the roles of the other members. This enables all of them to work without crossing other members' boundaries. It avoids the classic role confusion messages: 'Sorry, didn't know you were doing that', or 'Sorry, thought that was someone else's job!'

The boundaries need to be defined and agreed

The time-scale of the commitment required from the team, the frequency and actual dates of team meetings, what members can expect from the team leader by way of communication, and so on, are all discussed and agreed, and members leave to begin their various jobs feeling that they belong to a team that has a clear purpose, and is safe because the team leader is holding the boundaries.

The team leader needs to maintain continuing contact with each of the members of the team between meetings. This could be by a regular weekly telephone call, or (considerably less effective) by the circulation of minutes. Quite often things that seemed crystal clear during a meeting become uncertain afterwards, and team members almost always need encouragement and support to clarify their own roles once they have left the reinforcing boundaries of the team meeting. Team-building is a task in itself, and is vital if the communication task is to be achieved.

BRAINSTORMING THE TEAM

It can sometimes be a great help for the second part of an inaugural meeting to have a brainstorming session where the whole team is asked to suggest ideas about how the task should be achieved. All sorts of ideas can flow from this, many of which will be discarded. But some will almost certainly emerge as 'brilliant', and can be adopted. Not only that, but each member will feel that he or she has contributed not only to his or her own role, but to the task as a whole.

It is often during such 'brainstorming sessions' that the most creative ideas are born. People's enthusiasm is at its maximum at the start of the project, and they feel less restricted by other people's power or skills, or by the sheer process of the team.

AGREEING A MANAGEMENT SYSTEM

It will help each member of the team if they know exactly who is responsible for what. For example, if there is money to be spent on design, or on attitude monitoring, then those members of the team who have responsibility for these areas need to know how to get authority to spend money. Do they simply need to ask the project treasurer, or should each expense be agreed at a team meeting? Does the team leader want to agree expense requests with the project treasurer? What about design decisions? Should these be presented to the team?

These are all matters which relate to the boundaries of each of the roles, and might surface when the roles are initially discussed. But an inexperienced team (or team leader) may forget them initially, so it helps to have the management structure as a specific item on the agenda.

The team leader needs to make it quite clear to the team exactly what the boundaries of his or her responsibilities are. By taking responsibility for the project, and for the team, the members can feel safer and therefore more able to be creative. But the team leader should also make it possible for any team member to feel able to raise problems. A statement along the following lines can help:

'I have found that in all projects like this, unforeseen problems can arise. If any problems do arise, they belong to the whole team, and not just to the individual member who discovers them. So, please, let me know the moment you think you might have discovered or even created a problem. We will then work together to resolve them. No one should feel that they have a problem which they cannot share, and I am always available on the phone to discuss difficulties.'

WORKING TO AN AGENDA

An agenda is like a map: it can help the team leader to cover those things that need to be covered, and it helps each member to feel that they know where they are. Simple, unspoken questions like 'How much longer are we going to be here?' can block people's attention and energy, but if they have an agenda which shows that they are two thirds through the business they can make their own assessment.

But agendas are only as good as the chairmen or chairwomen who run the meeting. You can have a great agenda, covering all the ground, but if you fail to move off item one people will get restless. Try to have at least some idea of the timescale of your agenda in your mind. It rarely helps to make the timing public knowledge, because if you get time slippage on one item people will feel frustrated, not knowing that you intend to make up time on a later item.

28 IMAGE AND MYTH

The desire for perfect communication between individuals and societies is probably as old as the human race itself. The expression of that desire and its frustration finds its place in one of the oldest stories of the Bible. In the account of the building of the Tower of Babel, there is a real attempt to grapple theologically with the fact that the variety of languages found amongst the races and nations of God's world in itself creates misunderstanding and is often a root cause of division. However, like so many of the teaching stories of the Bible, the ancient theologian constructed a parable that goes much further, and points to the direct link between communication and power.

In this particular story, the inability to engage in effortless and transparent communication with the rest of the human race is part of God's protection of his creation. Only thus can he protect it from both the folly and deliberate evil of fallen humanity. Had we the ability to communicate at will with whoever we wanted, the power that this would give us to corrupt and destroy would be a far greater potential evil than the misunderstandings caused by our inability to communicate well. In fact, the necessity of having to work 'by the sweat of your brow' at communication is both part of the curse of Adam, and also part of the suffering involved in the redemptive process.

It is fascinating that this desire for total, transparent communication surfaces in every generation, and is often expressed both in popular literature and in the technological drive. In our own age, the 'Gaia mythology', where each atom of matter is linked to all the others at a level of consciousness where each knows, and is known by, the other, is more than mere science fiction: it is a repeat of the old Babel, but without any recognition of the potency or effect of evil or of humankind's fallen nature.

However you interpret the theology of communication, it is an incontrovertible part of the nature of humanity that all communication is partial, imperfect and, in many cases, misleading. Someone once set out the rule that any fault in communication lies with the communicator: a useful rule in so far as it places responsibility for accurate communication with the communicator, and avoids blaming the recipient. But life isn't that simple. Even the best communication will be contaminated by a host of difficulties which lie in the gap between the communicator and the recipient.

The human mind is not comfortable with incomplete pictures. It can hold any number of different or even contradictory pictures and arguments at the same time provided that they are more or less complete in themselves. But where there are gaps of information that are wide enough to draw attention to themselves, the human mind will try to fill in those gaps by drawing on previous experience and current belief systems to 'create' a complete image which, while it may well differ from, or directly contradict, other images, will at least have its own internal completeness.

By 'image', we mean the perception held by people about the source of the image. For example, a photographic slide generates an 'image' of the photograph when a light is shone through it. The 'image' may be more or less clear depending on whether it is 'focused' correctly.

Equally, the 'image' of a local church held in the minds of people living in the local community may be more or less accurate depending on the information they have received, their own bias, and the information that is generated by that church. The task of the Christian communicator is to ensure, as far as possible, that the 'image' of that church is as accurate, as faithful to the reality, as possible.

Sometimes a communicator is asked to improve the 'image' of an organization or community in a way that distorts its reality. This temptation to create an illusion rather than reality, is what has given a bad name to public relations. If the source is poor, its image will be poor. The answer is not to create a falsely 'improved' image, but to improve the source itself.

Perhaps this is best explained by a modern parable. A man was giving a party, but was unhappy about the decoration of his house. He strung up some fairy lights, moved his furniture so that the holes in the carpet were hidden, and turned down the main lights. The illusion of beauty was created. But when most of the guests had arrived, someone came into the room and switched on the main light. Immediately the illusion was spoiled. The holes in the carpet were revealed, and the stain on the curtains showed up.

There were two choices. One was to react angrily and to switch off the light as quickly as possible. The other was to clean up the room.

When the Christian communicator is asked to deal with issues of image, there are times when the source itself needs to change. The issues can then be as much about repentance as they can be about communication!

The problem for the communicator is that the image produced may, or may not, be an accurate reflection of the truth. A false image might prevent me from receiving messages which contradict it, even if those messages convey the truth. If my 'image' of the church is a picture of half a dozen elderly ladies wrapped up in overcoats, worshipping in a cold, dark church built to hold over a thousand people, I will find it hard to receive any coherent messages about a youth service. In fact, I will probably interpret the messages in the context of the 'image' I already hold, and will either dismiss them because they conflict with that image, or will simply be unable to receive them.

Each of us has a complex set of 'images' within which we make sense of all the messages we receive. Associated with these images are certain key words which trigger them. To see what I mean, look at the following list of key words and see what pictures, what 'images' form in your mind:

police

library

family

church

work

hospital

dentist

baby

ballet

holiday

politician

public house.

Each of us will have a particular set of images which we associate with key words, and those images may be pleasant or unpleasant, true or false. In fact, the images we have are distinctively 'ours': they are what make us the type of person we are, because we use this set of images against which to test the messages we receive. If, for example, my image of 'dentist' involves pain and fear, I will relate any message about dentists to this image, and interpret it accordingly. If, however, my image of 'dentist' involves the relief of pain or discomfort, and is warm and comforting, it will enable me to receive and interpret messages about dentists in a much more positive way.

The difficulty for the communicator is that, by using particular words to communicate, we are attempting to evoke a particular image or set of images in our listeners, and to use their images as common ground on which to communicate. If, however, the image evoked in our hearers is an image which is substantially different from the image we are using to generate or nurture the message, then we are immediately in danger of mis-communicating.

Nowhere is this danger more apparent than with religious language. Not only do we use words to connect our messages to images which are commonly shared with those who do not hold our beliefs, but, because of the nature of religious truth, we often use words to construct whole new stories, pictures, poetry or images through which we convey truth or meaning about ourselves or our beliefs. In one breath we use language linked to commonly held images such as 'washing' or 'feeding'; but in the next we link these words to a framework of images that is constructed from a very specific and particular religious experience.

Take one simple example. The huge difficulty of describing specific communication between God and individual people has led to the development of a set of images surrounding the concept of 'the messenger', a term which is rendered in New Testament Greek as *angelos*, or 'angel'. The angel is variously described in scripture in images which range from a stranger indistinguishable from any other person to a feathered creature with wings and a human body. The Christmas-tree angel bears little resemblance to the biblical 'messenger', but its image is so well fixed in the minds of most of our hearers that it would be a brave communicator who used the imagery of angels in today's media!

Part of the task of the communicator must therefore be one of deconstruction. Those false images that have been formed in either the individual or the corporate mind may need to be shattered, or at least gently dismantled, before the more important messages can help to form the more accurate image by which the individual or community can respond to the truth communicated through the Word made flesh.

For the average church communicator, there are two important ways by which false or misleading images can be deconstructed:

◆ by supplying correct information to fill the gaps

◆ by challenging the false assumptions on which an image is built.

A good practical example of the first is found in the action taken by one local church following an informal survey of those living in its catchment area. It was a lively church, full to the brim with children of primary school age and below. There were masses of activities for this age group—and a waiting list for most of them. However, when householders with little or no contact with the local church were asked what the church could be providing for them, many replied that they wanted some activities for young children!

Clearly, there was an 'image' problem. The image of the church in the minds of the respondents did not include weekday activities for children, and without a knowledge of what was happening, they had built up a picture of the local church which was for adults only. The church took corrective action. They published a newsletter with lots of photographs of their work with young children, together with articles about the church which highlighted that work, and distributed it free around the estates. They repeated this three times throughout the year. The result was a change of perception, and the need for a bigger church building!

29 TAIL PIECE

Theory is all very well, but until it is put into practice, it belongs to someone else. The purpose of this book has been to set out a practical, step-by-step approach to improving the internal and external communications of a local church or congregation. It will have achieved its purpose only if it encourages its readers actually to make a start in applying the information. Whilst most of us want to be sure that we have mastered a skill completely before we expose ourselves to the risk of failure or ridicule through putting it into practice, it is a vain hope.

One of my grumbles about house groups is that they are the biggest excuse I know for not doing anything. It is possible to learn by sitting in comfortable armchairs, week after week, sharing other people's experiences. But it is far better to go out and get your own experience by trying to feed the hungry, clothe the poor, house the homeless or visit the prisoner. After all, Jesus didn't say 'Take, understand.' He said 'Take, eat.'

In fact, most of our learning comes through our own experience, or at least through a reflection on our own experience. Our failures will lead to a change of practice, or to a different way of doing things. Our successes will spur us on to a bigger vision for what is possible. Yet the scriptures tell us that all things are possible for the servants of the King, and that he will take our smallest efforts and weave them into the seamless pattern of his kingdom.

So whether it's a matter of taking a deep breath, lifting the phone, and speaking to the news editor of the local newspaper or radio station, or whether it's putting together a tentative communications plan for your church's mission, there is nothing achieved at all unless you make a start.

FOR A BETTER WORLD

Richard Adams and Phil Wells

A discussion-leading-to-action guide for those who want to take informed social action

£8.00
ISBN 0 7459 2682 7

YOUTHWORK, AND HOW TO DO IT

Sam Adams, Judith Levermore and Pete Ward

The Oxford Youth Works guide to working with young people.

'I am greatly impressed by the innovative and visionary ministry of Oxford Youth Works.'

Dr George Carey

£8.00
ISBN 0 7459 2879 X

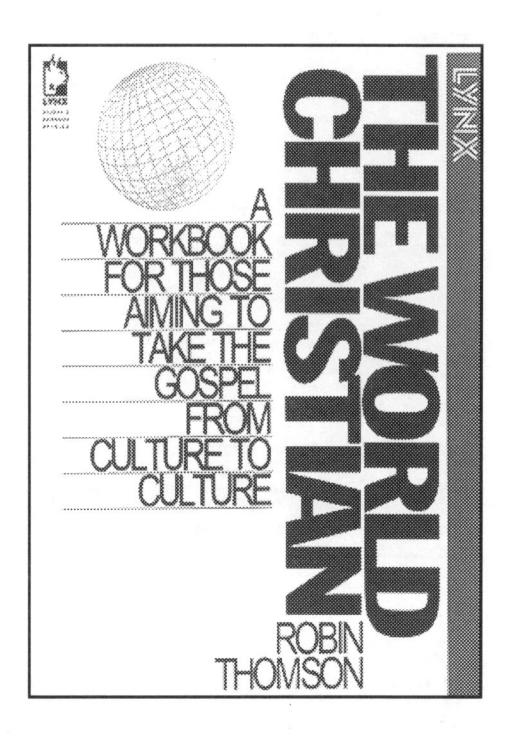

THE WORLD CHRISTIAN

Robin Thomson

A worbook for those aiming to take the gospel across cultural boundaries

£10.50
ISBN 0 7459 2540 5

DANCING IN THE DARK?

The main seminar notes from Spring Harvest 94, covering the topic of the church, and based on the Letter to the Philippians, give churches and groups the chance to link their own programme with the central activity of these massively popular conferences

£6.00
ISBN 0 7459 3030 1

GOOD NEWS DOWN THE STREET: CHURCH PRESENTATION PACK

Michael Wooderson

All you need to explain this tried-and-tested method to church members. Contains video, audio-cassette, photocopy mastersheets and booklets.

£40.00 inc VAT
ISBN 0 7459 2772 6

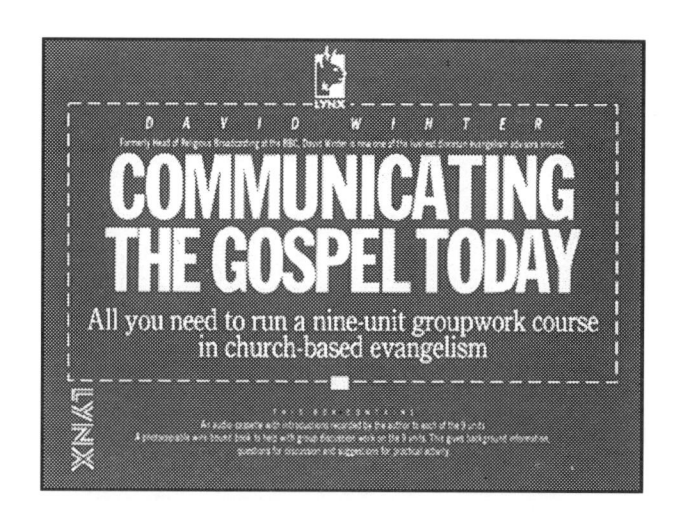

COMMUNICATING THE GOSPEL TODAY

David Winter

All you need to run a nine-unit groupwork course in church-based evangelism. Contains audio-cassette introductions and manual.

£20 inc VAT
ISBN 0 7459 2691 6

These books are available from your bookshop or direct from:

Lynx Communications,
Peter's Way,
Sandy Lane West,
Oxford, OX4 5HG,
England

or fax with your credit card number:

UK: 0865 747568
International: +44 865 747568

Add for postage and packing:

£1 (UK)
£3 (Europe)
£5 (Rest of the world)